The Smell of Evangelism

Chaplain William Dillon

The Smell of Evangelism

By Chaplain William Dillon

ISBN: 9781712222959

Edited by Cindy Moore

Cover Design by Cindy Moore

For information about chaplain training and endorsement or to order books by William Dillon, please go to website or communicate by email using the contact information below.

Web Site: www.ocachaplains.com

Email: William@plisolutions.com

Printed in USA

Dedication

To my best friend and helpmeet, my wife, Gwenlyn Ree Dillon. She has been my best supporter and encourager for over forty-five years. Gwen is the smartest, most level-headed and kind person that I know. She has talents so great that she is probably the only one in the world that cannot see them.

To my son Shannon who gave me the title for this book when he was the first to ask why my Bible smelled like cigarette smoke to which I replied, "That is the smell of evangelism."

To all my children and especially those who I dragged to every home Bible study and event while helping others. Their giving nature has also helped me write this book.

To my daughters-in-law who are the best daughters-in-law in the world, and my son-in-law who is the best bi-lingual preacher in the world.

To all my grandchildren who are the smartest and best-looking in all the world.

Acknowledgements

To those authors, representatives, and publishers who have allowed us to use their work without charge; to those who allowed us special arrangement, and to those whose work is now in the public domain, we are grateful.

The author has made every effort to trace the authorship of all selections and direct quotes and give proper credit through citation. When no name appears the authorship is unknown.

Much of the information contained in this book, was gained from education, seminars, books, instructors, lectures, and people with whom the author associated. This book is the sum total of all of the above.

Acknowledgement is made to the following who have contributed to the publication of this book.

My wife, Gwenlyn, who read through my many earlier drafts.

Cheryl Roye who helped with most of the second proofing.

Cindy Moore who did the bulk of hard work by bringing an order and flow to the book, and doing the final proofing, editing, and layout.

My friend, Eric Wiggins, who wrote the Foreword to this book.

My friend, Jim Williams, who wrote a Guest Testimony and recommendation for this book.

My friend, Sidney L. Poe, PhD, and Education Director of the Occupational Chaplains Association (OCA) who wrote a recommendation for this book.

The Mississippi Christian Writer's Association for their help and encouragement.

To my pastors Rev. Smith, Rev. Drury, Rev. Walker and Rev. Robbins who have spoken words of wisdom into my life, helping to make me into the person I am.

James Richardson who was my Clinical Pastoral Education (CPE) instructor and gave me permission to use the House Model in this book.

Table of Contents

Foreword

Just as you are...

We sing a song in my church choir, "Just as you are." It is a beautiful picture of how no matter where one is, God is ready, waiting and willing to take us - just as we are.

I am so thankful that Jesus took me just as I am. But he didn't stop there. He compels me to keep coming back to him daily just as I am, so that he may continually renew and bring about change in my heart and life. He will keep doing this for as long as I am willing to keep coming to him and until I am on high with him.

It's one thing for Christ to offer this to man. It is quite another for a man to be so giving to his fellow man. You see, it's easy to love, care, and counsel those that look the part, play the part, and never seem to need anything other than a Sunday morning smile. It is very different to go into the highways and hedges and get into the nooks and crannies of life to help people dig out, root out, and climb out of life's traps.

My friend, Bill Dillon, has the kind of heart for people that is extraordinary. He is not proud and puffed up. He is a humble man whose love for people and genuine desire to care and help cannot be missed.

I first met him while he was representing a workplace chaplain ministry team my workplace used. I was responsible for employee benefits and as such I worked closely with Bill. I never found his business practices to be any different than his chaplaincy practices. He was (and is) honest, trustworthy, caring and dedicated.

Later, I knew Bill as a close friend and confidant. I suffered through some deeply personal troubles, and Bill looked beyond the face that I put on at work and looked into my heart. He gently nudged and prayed and extracted tiny pieces of brokenness from somewhere deep within me to help me as I turned to God to help me make it through those dark days.

Bill masterfully expanded his heart of ministry through work in his local church, prisons, the local community and many local workplaces. In doing so, he much enlarged the "congregation," to which he was deeply devoted.

I have observed him build up people, counselors, chaplains, ministers and champions of the faith everywhere from the halls of government to the aisles of factories.

If you are looking for wisdom, guidance or advice about how to serve as a chaplain, look no further than Bill Dillon. While his degrees and education are more akin to those from the school of hard knocks than a university, he possesses a balanced educational background that when mixed with the perfume of years of real life experience creates an aroma you cannot and do not want to miss.

I trust this book blesses you as it has me, and I am so thankful to my dear friend for sharing it with me - and you.

Eric Wiggins

Guest Testimony

Product of Chaplaincy…

I am a product of the chaplaincy ministry. Chaplain William Dillon, whose services were provided by my employer, demonstrated caring kindness to my wife during her final struggles in this life and compassion to me and my family on her passing. The result was that I became a member of the church he pastored, and have been used by God in healings and the conversion of many to the faith.

Before meeting Bro. Dillon, I had been a denominational Christian with a strong faith in God. I had attended church every time the doors were open, taught Sunday School, and had been involved in soul winning. Unfortunately, my test of faith occurred when my wife Judy was diagnosed with rheumatoid arthritis and her health began to fail. I did not do well with the process that was attacking my wife and love of my life. I began to question God and later pulled away from Him in my anger at Him. The disease which we discovered when Judy was twenty-nine years old, progressively destroyed her body despite many surgical procedures to keep her life quality at the highest possible.

Meanwhile, in the years after our discovery of my wife's disease, I applied myself to my career which began as an engineer in the defense industry and progressed through ever increasingly responsible jobs to Director of Manufacturing. As the defense industry began to decline, I changed industries holding the Plant Manager position in three commercial products companies and finally secured a position as the Plant Manager of a cable manufacturing company in Arkansas where I first met Bro. Dillon in 2004. Bro. Dillon was the lead chaplain for our company. I must add that after a brief conversation with Bill, I avoided him like the plague on his weekly visits to the plant (people who are backsliders like I was are not at all comfortable around those serving God).

My wife took a major turn for the worse in early 2005, and we were forced to hire a day nurse to help while I worked. God was certainly in the selection of the nurse; she was a member of Bro. Dillon's church, and with my wife's permission, Bro. Dillon and Mrs. Dillon came to our house and prayed with her several times. In November 2005, after another surgery, my wife had an infection that put her in a coma. Driving her one hundred twenty (120) miles to a major hospital in Shreveport, LA (I had no confidence that our local medical professionals and hospital could help her), the infection was discovered, and three days later she awoke. We were there for ten more days. Each and every day, Bro. Dillon called to check on her and usually offered to come there.

Once released to go home, under the advice of the doctor, Judy was placed into the hospice program. Days later she told me to have Bro. Dillon come to our house when I would be home. That Thursday evening, when Bro. Dillon made his visit, I was shocked at Judy's request of him, and I remember her words exactly, "Bro. Dillon, I am not going to live much longer, and when I die, I want you to preach my funeral." I don't remember much else of that meeting... it was short and to the point. Judy passed away during the early morning hours six days later at the age of fifty-seven.

The first one on the scene at my house, after I called work to report the passing of my wife on December 15, was Bro. Dillon at around nine a.m. As I remember, Bill said very little but offered to call people I needed to notify and let me tell them the news. He didn't have to say anything; his presence as one who had demonstrated many times that he cared was enough. Sometimes a grieving person just needs the comfort of a friend's presence and no words. We had coffee but pretty much sat there between visits by friends and colleagues as I set up the necessary tasks around the funeral. At around two p.m. I thanked Bro. Dillon, provided directions to the little country church one hundred fifty (150) miles away, packed my bag and went to meet my children who were driving to my father's home in north Louisiana from Florida and Georgia. Bro. Dillon was at the little church where my grandfather, grandmother, uncle, and mother had their funerals for the Friday evening visitation and to preach a message of hope on Saturday morning, leaving after the burial and church-provided lunch; he declined my offer for payment for his services. My children and I left for my home later that afternoon.

The next day my son and I went to the church where Bro. Dillon was pastor for my sole purpose of giving an offering (since Bill would not take my offering after the funeral!). I thought this would probably be my first and last visit to this church! The next week Bro. Dillon invited me to Sunday service and lunch with him and his family. I was still very appreciative for his ministry to my wife and to me after she was gone, so I went back to his church and to a very enjoyable after-church meal. He told me Sister Freeman would be coming to the church for Friday through Sunday services in the near future. Sister Freeman who I had not met but my wife had spoken excitedly about, had been to my house with Bro. Dillon to pray for Judy in August. I decided I wanted to hear her. Not long after going to these meetings, I had a three-hour Bible Study with Bro. Dillon with respect to "the Baptism of the Holy Ghost." I wanted my faith to rise to the level I saw in him and some members of his congregation. I began to pray and study the book of Acts each evening after work. I received the baptism of the Holy Ghost on the evening of January 28, 2006, which was forty-five days after the passing of my wife and the day before what would have been our thirty-ninth anniversary.

Since that evening, I came to call William Dillon "my pastor" as a member of the church he pastored. I began going to Sunday afternoon Jail ministry and took over the leadership of that ministry soon after. With God's leadership, I received my Local License from the United Pentecostal Church in 2008 and my General License in 2010. I became a certified Anger Management instructor for our local ministry for people convicted of substance abuse crimes and anger related crimes and those who were ordered into the programs. God has used me to lead dozens of people to repentance and baptism in the name of Jesus in both the local jail and at the Mississippi State Penitentiary at Parchman including several on Death Row. I have seen our Lord heal or extend the lives of many people when I have prayed for them. I have been honored by my Lord Jesus to baptize hundreds of converts in the precious name of Jesus Christ. Without the services of a caring chaplain in my wife's and her family's lives at our time of need, this would never have happened.

Jim Williams

Preface

Blurring the lines of chaplaincy is one tool that has given me a wide-open field of labor. I have been a Christian Prisoner Fellowship (CPF) chaplain, a state and regional director for CPF, a police chaplain, a corporate chaplain, and a hospital chaplain. I have also worked as a Justice Court chaplain and a chaplain in nursing homes, drug rehabs, and federal halfway houses. Additionally, I am a Drug and Alcohol Instructor and an Anger Management Instructor. Having worked in many areas of chaplaincy has increased my access to people in every kind of situation.

When I was a corporate chaplain, I had someone I was helping in the hospital. Since I was also a hospital chaplain, I was given access to many people at the hospital. Having the codes to the emergency room and restricted areas gave me freedom to help in anything related to medical emergencies. If a patient had a family member in jail, since I was already set up with both the local sheriff and police departments, I had access to minister there as well. It is easy to see the advantages of these crossover patterns. Being a chaplain for the court system, many times I was allowed to help in a domestic arrest or drug arrest by offering Drug and Alcohol training or Anger Management training in lieu of a jail sentence.

When I started in the ministry, I had never been taught anything about how to help people as a pastor. I did not really know the proper way to meet their emotional and spiritual needs; I was taught how to communicate with God and to preach and teach, but nothing about helping in crisis situations. I believe the kind of information in this book is needed for anyone who is a caregiver in ministry. Whether it be as a chaplain, a pastor, a youth pastor, a volunteer at a jail, a home missionary, an inner city missionary, an evangelist, a children's home worker, or the listener on the end of a hotline, you are an emotional and spiritual caregiver. I say caregiver because care is what is given. Caregivers should also give love, compassion, and their ears.

The reason I started searching for answers began with an accident I happened upon when I was on my way to work as a bi-vocational pastor in the mountains of Washington state. A girl was trapped inside her car, and because I did not know what to do, and others with more training said to leave her alone until the ambulance arrived, I backed off. The girl was sitting straight up with her seatbelt on, but the roof had caved in, pushing her head down and cutting off her breathing. Ten minutes went by before the first responders arrived. It was quickly realized that the jaws-of-life needed fuel. They had to flag down a passing log truck to get some gas. All of this took several more minutes before they could cut her loose. She took a huge gulp of air when they freed her but died two weeks later. I said I would never again be untrained when encountering another crisis.

Determined to learn how to help and how to be a caregiver, I began to self-educate by going to seminars, taking courses, reading and researching. I became involved more deeply in ministry, becoming a chaplain. I kept learning. I've been involved in ministry and have been a chaplain for forty years. I love people. I want to pass what I have learned to others. I trust you will find the information and stories beneficial to your ministry as a spiritual caregiver.

Chaplain William Dillon

Introduction

From the start, I would like to say this is not meant to be a scholarly book, as there are many great works on the subject of chaplaincy and their efforts. Rather, I wanted to bring a down-to-earth approach to chaplaincy and ministry in general. Although I have pastored churches, most of my ministry life has been as a chaplain of some kind or another; therefore, I refer to chaplaincy the most. From my personal experience, I hope to communicate and convey what it takes to enter into or be successful in this special field of ministry or any field of ministry, because all of the information herein applies.

I am currently the director for Occupational Chaplains Association. Our mission is to train and endorse chaplains. At the time of this writing, we have about three hundred (300) endorsed chaplains across the United States.

I remember a training seminar Dr. Sidney Poe and I held in Texas. Dr. Poe is our director of education for training and preparing people to minister as emotional and spiritual caregivers. There were several dozen potential chaplains in attendance, soaking up everything being taught. On this particular day, we invited a successful, professional chaplain to teach. I will call him "Chaplain Ron." When Chaplain Ron began his portion of the training, it soon became evident that his path to becoming a paid chaplain had been long and hard. The more he talked, the more the trainees' hope of becoming a chaplain weakened. He spoke of eight years of college and years of chaplain training. It was my unfortunate duty to be the next presenter, and I thought, "What can I say that will bring hope back to these trainees?" I prayed earnestly about it because he had even discouraged me even though I had been a chaplain for years. When I got up, I said, "Wow, I sure am glad I did not meet

Chaplain Ron before I started chaplain ministry. I would have never become a chaplain." This broke the tension, and the class revived. The truth of the matter is that while a great education is wonderful, the majority of people will never go back to college to get their master's degree or Doctorate in Divinity. Most people cannot quit their jobs and go back to college for years, just to be able to help others, and yet the world is dying because there are not enough workers in the harvest.

I did not receive the Holy Ghost until I was twenty-seven years of age. I had not gone to church for eleven years, but when God was merciful and saved me, I hit the ground running. Within a month of my conversion, I was preaching the gospel. With a wife and children to support, I had no time to go back to school. I had to work, and work I did. Isn't it kind of funny how nowadays you have to have a college degree to bury someone, but years ago all you had to have was a strong back, a shovel, and a bit of carpentry knowledge to make a pine box. I would never turn down the opportunity to gain more education, but it is truly sad to see a world being lost because caring people are so often required to have a Master's degree.

When I first became a chaplain I did not even know that I was doing chaplain ministry. I had no training; I only had a calling to minister to my fellow man. At that time, I was the youth pastor and a licensed minister in our local church. I volunteered at our local Union Gospel Mission. It was a short-stay mission much like the Salvation Army model, only all of the churches in the city supported it. Each church would take turns preaching to the temporary residents who were in need of shelter, and after the service, we would provide them a meal. I later became the interim director of the mission and then the president of the board of directors. When I started, it was a "men's-only" program, but we were eventually able to add a battered women's program during my time as president.

CPE (Clinical Pastoral Education) is the standard for most hospitals to obtain a paid position as a chaplain. Each unit is four hundred hours, one hundred hours of classroom time and three hundred hours of practicum. There are five units to most CPE programs. There are two main accepted CPE programs at this time, and most hospitals accept one but not the other. You would be wise to research what your local area hospitals accept if you are looking for a paid chaplain ministry position. I will be sharing some of my experiences and education from the CPE program that I was fortunate to take.

It is my hope to inspire others either already working as a chaplain in the harvest field, or those anticipating a harvest ministry. It is my desire that anyone involved in ministry of any kind where they might be called upon to be an emotional or spiritual caregiver, will learn from the information I have provided.

Orientation

Most states require a person to go through an orientation class in order to minister in a jail or prison, whether they are a licensed minister or volunteer. A mandatory background check is also required. If God has called you to this unique mission field, you need to be equipped.

Orientation is always a necessary but boring event, especially after the first dozen times you have been through it. The repetitiveness is necessary because of all the new workers that we have each year. Orientation informs us what the rules are, how to stay out of trouble, and what to do in an emergency. One thing to keep in mind is that no matter how many times a chaplain has been to a prison or a jail, one must listen to what the officers have to say. Many times when arriving at a state prison, we will be informed that a certain unit is on lockdown because of a stabbing or a murder the week before. After prayer, sometimes we will be allowed in to minister to the lockdown area. Other times we have to bypass that unit.

When locked in with a multitude of inmates, it is never one hundred percent safe; there are precautions to take. Although we believe in God's protection, and in the twenty-two years I have been going, I have never had a problem, we still do everything possible to keep risk at a minimum. For example, one thing we are never allowed to wear is a necktie as it would be too easy for a prisoner to grab it and gain quick physical advantage. An inmate could drag you into the bars or use it to choke you. Orientation is a very important part of keeping you safe, out of trouble, and able to come back to minister again. By following the rules, you will build trust with the prison or jail administration and with the inmates to whom you will be ministering.

Chaplain Ministry to the Incarcerated

Healing

"I am going to heal people in this revival", is what I believe God had spoken to me. The place was a large sprawling state prison with many smaller prison units. The occasion was a three-day annual revival. At that time, they separated the HIV and AIDS positive inmates into an area of their own. It was into this sub-prison that our group went to minister on a very hot humid day. The flies and mosquitoes played no favorites when landing on or biting everyone present. Trusting God to protect us, we stood among a group of approximately forty men and preached the healing power of Jesus, the power of His blood, and the remission of sins. We declared to them God was going to heal that day. Knowing the nature of their sicknesses and how they had become infected might have made their situation seem daunting, disheartening, and formidable, but we believed what God had spoken to us. At the end of the service, we laid hands upon the heads of many and prayed the prayer of faith. We then held another service where several repented and were baptized in Jesus's name, their sins forgiven and washed away.

As we left, I told the Lord, "I believe you healed people today, but I want to be able to tell others you healed; I need to have a witness." A few months later, I was telling this same story in a large church in the southern part of our state. We told how we went into the AIDS unit and that God had healed people in that unit. Afterwards, a woman met me and asked if I had gone into the HIV and AIDS unit at the state prison. I said, "Yes, we went into that unit and God healed people that day!"

She said, "I know that God healed people that day!" I asked her how she knew and she responded, "My brother was in that unit. He had gone away from God and fell into a terrible life-style where he contracted HIV. God healed him that day, and they had to move him out of that unit."

> I know that God healed people that day.

Spirits

Spirits are present in prisons in concentrated numbers. In one lockdown area, there was such confusion when we entered that it sounded more like wild animals than humans. The shouting and cursing from one level to another and back again was so intense, you could feel the air charged with viciousness. We stopped and prayed before continuing, and immediately the atmosphere changed.

I have also seen great calm suddenly come over an area when we walked into it. One day we went into death row, and Bro. John, who was such an anointed singer, was with us. When he began to sing, suddenly the whole atmosphere changed, so much so that even the guards came running in to listen and feel the presence of God. In the next area of death row, there were spirits that did not like us. Erupting from two different cells, men began to howl off-key like dogs.

On another occasion, we were preaching in a jail, and a man started to fall out and have seizures or a fit of some kind. It seemed like more of an attempt to disrupt the service than a medical need, so we just went on with the service, and God healed people that day. We also baptized several from that service. One of our workers was unaware that we were ministering in the HIV/AIDS unit. When it came time to baptize, I happened to mention it. To say the least, there was a strong reluctance on his part to baptize them for fear of infection, but we finally moved ahead, knowing that the power of Jesus's name invokes the blood, not only for salvation, but also for healing. None of us became sick or contracted any disease.

Come out of the Wheelchair!

In the same year that God told us He was going to heal people, there was a young man who came to a prison service in a wheelchair. He had been in that condition since he was seven. That night he got out of his wheelchair completely healed. Due to time constraints and rules placed on us by the prison, he was whisked away right after service. I looked for him each time we went for the annual revival without finding him. In the third year following, we found him, and he was still walking and didn't need a wheelchair. He was waiting for us to baptize him in Jesus's name, which we did.

> That night he got out of his wheelchair completely healed.

Mighty Rain Stopped

In this particular prison, at certain times of the year, there are great rainstorms. So excessive is the rainfall, that at a specified point, they shut down the entire prison as a precaution to prevent inmates from escaping. With such heavy rain, it is impossible to see anything more than about fifteen feet away, so it would be useless trying to

track someone who had escaped. We were informed that one of these rainstorms was upon us and that we would have to shut down the revival. We had a group traveling from another city to sing; we were told, "You might as well tell them, don't come." There were about fifty of us altogether. We gathered into a large room and declared that we were going to call on God to stop this storm. You should have heard the outcry as these men and women reached up and caught the ear of God. Suddenly, the rain and the wind ceased, and we went on with the revival, baptizing dozens and seeing many filled with the Holy Ghost.

Greatest Move of God I Have Seen

Perhaps the greatest time I witnessed a sweeping move of God's Spirit was in our county jail. I had worked for many months preaching in two jails, the city and the county jails. Every week, we would have anywhere from three to six services in each facility. In the older jails, the guards would lock you in the pod with the inmates. We would have our service, and then they would let us out so we could go on to the next pod and do it all over again. Once, the guards changed shifts and failed to tell the oncoming shift-guards that I was in a cell, so no one came to let me out. Finally, I had to place a collect call to someone who called my wife. She called the sheriff's department and said, "Let the preacher out." They came and let me out so I did not have to spend the night in jail. After ministering for many months and having baptized about eighty-five inmates, no one had yet received the Holy Ghost. I remember

praying for God to send someone to help break through this wall. The district CPF chaplain called me and said, "Why don't we have a Jail Blitz?" I asked him what that was, and he said that we would get a team together and hit both jails on the same day at the same time with revival services. So, we gathered a team together and scheduled with the jails. The director and I went to the city jail which held about twenty-five to thirty inmates in each pod. There was a walkway about three to four feet wide where we stood just outside the bars. When we started the service, there were about twelve men in the common area. We had a short song service, followed by preaching, and at the end, the director led them in a prayer of repenting and forgiving. Suddenly, the Holy Ghost fell on several of

23

them. There was such a surge of the Spirit of God that men were openly weeping and calling on God to forgive them. I was very happy that we had our first prisoners receive the Holy Ghost. God suddenly spoke to me and said, "Step back; you have not seen anything yet." I took only one step backward, and without warning, there was a rush of the Spirit that swept the whole pod. So strong was it that other men who had not attended came rushing out of their sleeping areas and fell against the bars weeping and repenting. Four more received the Holy Ghost right then. That day, we had seven receive the baptism of the Holy Ghost.

We were so excited that the next week we drove to a jail two hours away where another church had ministered for ten years without a Holy Ghost breakthrough. At the end of that service, we began to pray for the inmates. The first person we prayed for was a man convicted of murdering his best friend. He fell to the floor and received the Holy Ghost. The next six had the same experience, and we had another seven receive the Holy Ghost. The following week we returned to the county jail where we had worked for months, and seven more inmates received the Holy Ghost, bringing the total to twenty-one filled in three weeks.

Shortly after this, I became the prison chaplain for our state and led the annual crusades. I was not in this meeting of which I am about to tell you, as I was in another meeting in another part of the prison being conducted at the same time. One of our teams was having a service in one of the lock-down areas. These are areas that house those who are dangerous or who have committed violent crimes. They are locked down, one and two inmates to a cell depending on their level of risk. When it came time to baptize them, each inmate would be brought out one at a time with chains on their hands and ankles with another chain running between their hands and feet. On this day, we had an inmate who had repented and now was being baptized. When he went down into the water, he was shackled, but when he came up out of the water, his shackles were in the bottom of the tank, and his hands were raised as he received the Holy Ghost. Talk about surprised guards who were completely unnerved trying to figure out what had just happened and if there were going to be problems. No, there were no problems, but everyone there saw a miracle that day.

> ...when he came up out of the water, his shackles were in the bottom of the tank.

I once left my city about two hours before dawn and drove to the prisons to baptize some inmates. I had brought another man with me. We began to baptize in one prison compound, then moved our portable baptism tank to the next one and continued in this manner. When we were finished, we drove home and arrived after dark. I do not remember the exact number, but approximately seventy inmates were baptized that day. This was during the period when we were being opposed and harassed by the head chaplain who did not want us to baptize any inmates, so we had to do it several days after the crusade. He opposed us so that he could go in and try to baptize inmates before we could come back and do it. He did not like it that we baptized in Jesus's name.

We have also baptized many guards and had a positive effect on other staff chaplains. I remember that one of the prison staff chaplains confided to one of our team members that he was

25

addicted to pornography and asked for prayer. That same chaplain was with my team one year as we were escorted into each unit. After a service where he had felt the Holy Ghost, and when we were getting ready to leave for the day, he was standing next to our group in the parking lot when an idea struck me. I said, "Let's all join hands and pray." I prayed that he would feel the Holy Ghost. Suddenly, he began to jump and shake like a man who had taken hold of a live wire.

He said, "When I retire from my organization, I am going to become Pentecostal." He was in an organization that had no emotional demonstration in their religious rituals or practices.

Death Row Ministry

Death row is a great place to share the gospel. The inmates cannot leave their cells to attend services, so the only way for them to hear the Gospel message is for us to go to them. One time while in death row, the guard told us, "Do not go near the man in the corner." He was a large man, tall and stocky from what I could tell as he sat right next to the bars playing solitaire. He had nearly killed the head chaplain from this institution not long before. This same head chaplain had gone so far as to call the warden and complain about us. As director for our state prison ministry, I was called out of one of our services into the head chaplain's office where I was

confronted by the warden for the entire prison complex. This *prison farm* consisted of about twelve to fifteen separate prisons. I was caught completely off guard, not knowing what the head chaplain had told him about us, but from the warden's stern look, I knew it could not have been good. After some questioning, the reality of the matter came to light as the Lord gave me a response that caused the entire situation to come crashing down. I remember the look on the warden's face when I gave him the answers to his questions. He did not say anything to me but turned toward the head chaplain, as if to say, "That's not what you told me." From that moment on, we had no more problems for the remainder of our revival.

This same head chaplain had given our chaplains an incredible amount of trouble for years, trying to keep us from baptizing the inmates. We baptized as

many as one hundred sixty-eight in one of the revivals in the early years. The lowest I can remember being baptized was around sixty in the last few years. Many of the long-term inmates had been baptized already. Later directors had to go to the governor and to the head chaplain in charge of "all" the state prisons to resolve the conflict that this single prison chaplain had created concerning baptism. He kept up his attack on us but covered his tracks better for several more years.

Going back to the inmate on death-row that that nearly killed the chaplain, the inmate had said he did not want to see a chaplain, but the head chaplain went anyway. This broke the rules of the prison, not only nearly costing him his life, but also putting the guards in a dangerous situation trying to save him. Many prayers were answered that day, and that head chaplain is no longer employed at that prison. I guess this proves that even if you are in a senior position, breaking the rules has penalties.

Death Row Conversion

Our team of four went into death row one day and shared the

gospel with those inmates residing in their eight by twelve solitary cells. We met a man who had been transferred into this facility only two hours before. Upon hearing the Good News that his sins could be forgiven and washed away, he repented. A few hours later, we baptized him, and God filled him with His spirit. You never know the appointments that God sets up for you. You never know when you are the last person to minister to someone before eternity.

To illustrate this point further, I know of a person who went to a doctor's appointment. After the last patient was seen, the doctor my friend had seen earlier said good-bye to his staff and committed suicide. You just never know when you are holding the last thread of hope a desperate person needs.

What Can Be Forgiven?

In the story of Joseph, we find that God wanted to save the ten brothers as much as he did Joseph. The brothers were so full of hatred that they wanted to kill Joseph but ended up kidnapping and selling him as a slave. Hating enough to kill your own brother is caused by jealousy and envy. God sees each of our hearts as … *desperately wicked above all things* … (Jeremiah 17:9) As a result of what they had done, the ten brothers embarked on a low path of guilt-ridden years filled with sorrow and remorse. Their journey brought them years of broken and strained relationships, living with a lie. They must have felt like an animal that had fallen into a hunter's trap where they could not escape no matter how much they struggled. However, God was still wanting to save them as He had saved Joseph. When living with a lie, guilt, and the struggle to keep a past wrongdoing from coming to the surface while trying to keep it covered, there will often come a time when the secret will be revealed, frequently during a time of crisis. When Joseph's brothers went to Egypt and were accused of being spies and placed in prison, they remembered their past sin against Joseph. They confessed with their own mouths, …*We are verily guilty concerning our brother…therefore is this distress come upon us* (Genesis 42:21). Just as Joseph's brothers immediately attributed their demise to their past sin, oftentimes prisoners can see that what has happened to them is "just due" for crimes they have committed. It is at this point that it becomes possible for them to cry out to Jesus like the thief on the cross did. And what did Jesus do? He stopped in the very throws of death to comfort a man who was shortly going into eternity and in essence said, "I will save you."

Anger Out of Control

I know of a young man who had a successful business. Over the course of time, he became involved in a relationship with his secretary. Both of them left their spouses as they felt they were in love with each other. Jealousy began to work on the husband of the young lady until one day, his anger fully out of control, he showed up at her workplace and killed his former wife and the young man with whom she was involved. Afterward, he shot himself in the head. Somehow he lived, but I have since lost contact with the family, so I don't know if he ever became well enough to stand trial or go to prison. The point is this, what a sad ending to three lives. Crimes committed in this life against people and society must be punished, and while not excusing the horrible violent act of this enraged ex-husband, there is still a family shocked and hurting and a young man facing life with dire health issues and perhaps a prison sentence, if not the death penalty, all of whom need someone to minister to them.

Most people do not realize that murder is "The third leading cause of workplace death—behind "falls to a lower level" and "roadway collisions with other vehicles." This sobering data point comes courtesy of the latest Bureau of Labor Statistics study on fatal occupational injuries. What's behind all this…? News reports point to doomed love triangles and disgruntled co-workers."[1]

Having a chaplain in the corporate setting is one of the best ways to help prevent this.

I have spent many days and traveled hundreds of trips to our local jail visiting inmates I never knew. With one tragic occurrence, a person's life can be changed forever. I know of two church-

---

[1] James Graham, *The Killer in the Cubicle,* The Atlantic, October 2018. (https://www.theatlantic.com/magazine/toc/2018/10/)

attending young people whose lives were destroyed by jealousy. You say this doesn't happen in churches, but it does. Jealousy is as cruel as the grave. The emotions of the young man became so totally out-of-control, in a fit of rage, he took the young lady's life after she had broken off their relationship. I will never understand the mindset of someone who says, "I love you so much that I will kill you so no one else can have you if you don't want me." Now he sits in jail awaiting his many years in prison or possibly the death sentence, and her life has been literally destroyed, snuffed out in the prime of her life.

> ...in a fit of rage he took the young lady's life.

Several lives were ruined that day. I knew his pastor was not comfortable going to visit the young man, yet as wrong and hateful as he had been, he still needed someone to go talk to him about his soul. You can say that young man is not worthy of God's grace, and he should get everything he deserves. While I can agree that he should receive whatever punishment is imposed for his deeds, and that he is unworthy of God's grace, let me remind you that none of us is worthy of God's grace, and we also should have to pay the debt for our sins. Nonetheless, God extended to us forgiveness and grace, and He can extend it to this young man too.

Most times when I minister in a jail or prison, I never ask the inmate what they did to be placed there. Especially when I go on death row, I never ask. The only thing I want to do is show the love of God just like He did for me. After all, did not Jesus take time out from his dying to extend grace to a sinner and thief? I already gave an earlier example of a man on death row repenting, being baptized and filled with the Holy Ghost. This tells me that God wanted to forgive that man for whatever he had done that brought him to death row.

God Took Time for Murderers

It was Jesus who took time to minister to the thief hanging on the cross next to Him. God also went to Cain after he killed his own brother and spoke to him. We might wonder why that is and why God even cares about people who would do such terrible things. While I do not believe in being soft on crime or criminals, or that they need to escape their due punishment, I do believe in the mercy and grace of God. **1 Corinthians 6:11** says, ...*such were some of you.* I have to believe, but for the grace of God, it could be me. I am reminded that criminals were once someone's little child. I do not know what they have gone through, but they were made in the image of God Himself. I stand by my rule not to ask people why they are incarcerated and just share with them the love of God, unfettered by knowledge of their crimes.

The Smell of Evangelism

Dirty, hot and humid could not begin to give you an accurate picture of the county and city jails where I have ministered. A couple hundred men locked up with no air-conditioning and inmates smoking cigarettes produced quite a pungent smell. The cells were all in the middle with a small four-foot hall between individual cells and the outside wall. Here is where I would minister to inmates, leaning myself against the wall. One day one of the inmates shouted out, "Hey preacher! Watch out." As I quickly looked around, I saw a cockroach about three inches long moving rapidly on the wall heading straight toward me. Moving quickly, I denied the beast a place to hide in my clothing and went on with the service. In those days, the inmates were allowed to smoke, so even though the other smells were bad, the cigarette smoke was the worst. By the time I left the prison, after conducting five or six services, I smelled like a smoker for the rest of the day. The worst part wasn't just breathing the smoke or wearing it for the rest of the day, but my Bible took on the strong smell of cigarette smoke.

In our church we had several young men who were either lay ministers or wanting to be ministers. As I talked with them one day, I asked them if they knew what evangelism smelled like. Some were all ears, but others just looked at me as if I had just grown an extra head or something. One of them indicated that he wanted to know what evangelism smelled like. I opened my Bible and shoved it in his face and said, "Smell! This is what evangelism smells like."

> Smell! This is what evangelism smells like.

Evangelism the way the original church that the apostles established was not accomplished in nice fine environments. Evangelism was the preaching of the Gospel everywhere and in every perceivable venue of life.

Once I was teaching in a church I was pastoring about what it is to be a Christian and was speaking on the *aroma* of a Christian. I had hidden my bread-maker with bread baking in the baptistery before church. We went through the preliminaries of the service, and just as I began to teach, the bread maker began to send out the aroma of fresh-baked bread. It was a delicious smell that began to sweep through the church. Ladies began to nudge one particular sister known for cooking meals at church asking her what she had cooking. Pretending not to notice, I went on teaching on the aroma of a Christian. You see, while I believe that evangelism has one smell, the Christian has another. The aroma of a Christian should be a wonderful smell and a drawing smell emanating from his soul.

What does evangelism smell like? Like the sinful world we walk through if you are indeed like Jesus, a friend of sinners. What should a Christian smell like? Everything right and compelling, like hot bread just out of the oven, it will make you hungry.

Visionary Harvesters

The harvest is great but those who have a vision to do the work are still very few today. Why is this so? Jesus taught this concept over two thousand years ago. This is a command, a doctrine, and a prayer request of our Lord Himself. So what is the cause that the laborers remain few? I suppose there are several reasons. One to consider is that of being closed up inside church buildings since around three hundred (300) AD. Before that time, Christians did not have church buildings but were actively worshiping from house to house, giving them great access to the field. Yes, they went to the temple or synagogue when possible to pray or teach as Paul did, but most often they were turned away or persecuted by the very people who worshiped there.

Another reason the workers are few is the influence of old traditional religions that has blunted the understanding that launches workers. The work of the ministry was never intended to be narrowed to a few while leaving the masses of the army sitting in the church building. I know and recognize that much preaching, prompting, and even threatening has been carried out, trying to pry that army off its benches and pews. There are some churches that manage to break out and find innovative ways to get the army into the community, but it is not that way for the majority of churches. Over the years, I have heard it said that only fifteen percent of the congregation performs the work in a church. I have also heard the numbers argued that as high as twenty percent and as low as five percent are actual laborers in the church. In any case, the sad truth is that the vast majority are not in the field.

I once was told this story and do not know who wrote it, so I cannot rightfully give credit to its author. The story goes like this. There was a pastor that lived in a small, rural community. The deacons started to notice something strange that the pastor was doing. As they watched him, they thought they were seeing a troubling pattern, so they began to watch him carefully. Every day, around 4:30 p.m., the pastor would get in his car and drive out of town.

Later, he would come back with a big smile on his face. This bothered the deacons and they decided they needed to get to the bottom of it. One day, the leader of the deacon board decided to follow the pastor. The deacon observed as the pastor drove close to the railroad tracks, pulled his car over, and just sat there. Eventually a train passed by and the pastor watched it. After it was out of sight, he turned his car around and headed back to town. The deacon noticed that the pastor had a big smile on his face. This really puzzled the deacon because he was sure their pastor had been up to no good, and yet, all he was doing was looking at a train. There had to be something more going on. After all, a man does not act like this for no reason. After reporting

> ## There had to be something more going on.

back to the board and watching the same behavior many times, the deacons decided to ask the pastor about his strange behavior. They went to him and confessed sheepishly that they had been following him but could not understand what it was about the train that made him want to go out every day and watch it, and why did he always return with such a big smile? To this the pastor laughed and said, "It just makes me happy to watch something move that I don't have to push."

I wonder if this story originated from the cry of an overworked, burned-out pastor revealing his heart. Too many ministers are leaving the ministry each year because they are ministering in a way that was never Biblically intended. According to a New York Times article, "Members of the clergy now suffer from obesity, hypertension and depression at rates higher than most Americans. In the last decade, their use of antidepressants has risen, while their life expectancy has fallen. Many would change jobs if they could."[2]

---

[2] Paul Vitello, "Evidence Grows of Problem of Clergy Burnout," *New York Times,* 2 August 2010, Region section.

It is widely reported that somewhere around fifteen hundred (1500) clergy leave the ministry each month with some reports indicating the numbers to be even higher. I have read about research from some of the most respected research groups that back this up. I would recommend the book, *Leading on Empty*, by Wayne Cordeiro[3]. In his book, he tells how he ended up on a street curb crying uncontrollably at seemingly the height of what most considered a successful ministry. He was a mega-church pastor and a sought-after speaker. What could have caused such an episode?

This leads us to the third reason for few laborers and the thrust of this book. Many churches have moved away from the Biblical plan of the ministry and the equipping of the saints for the work of their ministry. The twofold problem lays in our lack of giving the tools to the laborers and helping them find their place in the harvest. Some just do not know how to equip their people with the tools to do the job. I know a very good pastor who made this statement to me, "No one ever taught me, so I cannot teach you." When I began to teach about chaplain tools, I recognized my own deficiency because no one had trained me.

Let's first address the tools needed for harvesters. As a pastor, I was lacking the tools myself to successfully help people in need. Within the circles where I ministered, I found no one teaching things like, *Sudden Unexpected Death Notification, Critical Incident Management, or Grief Ministry*. As a pastor I needed these kinds of tools to be effective in the ministry. What am I supposed to do, and what can I say during a death notification? As I began to self-educate, the doors began to open for me to teach others. A non-pastoral laborer may not ever be called on to do a death notification, but there are many other areas when dealing with people where training in grief handling, natural disasters and crises, or dealing with addiction problems can be utilized in supportive roles. There are a host of tools needed in today's world. People need ministered to during

---

[3] Wayne Cordeiro, *Leading on Empty*, (Bloomington, MN: Bethany House Publishers, 2009) 94

times of job loss, illness, accidents, bullying, hospitalization, and the list goes on and on. Many might say that this is the work of pastors. Why does the pastor have to make every hospital visit, be the only one to lift up every discouraged soul, attend every special event and plan every outing? Carrying all of the load for everyone is why so many pastors are suffering burnout. I submit to the reader that there are plenty of laborers to help the pastors when empowered and given the tools.

How does the ministering caregiver get out of the *got-to-do-everything* rut? It entails empowering others to do the work of the ministry and helping people find their place of labor in the harvest. They may never become a pastor, but that is not the goal. The book of Acts tells of Stephen who became one of the most effective deacons had by the early church. He went about healing the sick and serving the needs of the church, even giving his life for the gospel. When pastors empower people, delegate them, and apportion the workload, it allows them to multiply their God-given ministry and vision.

In my forty years of pastoral care, I have come to understand that not everyone is worthy of trusting with ministerial duties. In looking for harvesters, it is important to use people with a vision and encourage them to believe they can be helpful and that they are needed. This revelation comes with a spirit of fear which does not come from God. What has helped me overcome this is the knowledge that when God gives you something, there is no one on earth who can take that away. No saint or *ain't*, in or out of the

---

...when God gives you something, there is no one on earth who can take that away.

---

church, can steal what God has given. It might look like they can, but in the end they cannot. It looked like Absalom, King David's son, would be able to take the kingdom from David, but he was not able to do so because God had given it to David. Your vision cannot be taken away from you or others who are empowered to do God's work.

As you continue reading this book, my hope is that you will see the great need for training. Allow your heart to be open to an approach that will launch thousands into the harvest field. Allow your calling to permit you to see the need for others to work beside you in the harvest.

I make no apologies for writing this book from a Christian perspective as that would be disingenuous of who I am and what I believe. However, as a chaplain I have, I can, and I will minister to all people of all faiths, creeds, and even those without Christian faith. Ministering to all is the duty of everyone in ministry, but we must stay within the limits of the Bible, our convictions, and work in harmony with our church leadership. People are not won to Christ by force or theological battles, but by love. Our world is a platform for people to live out their Christian love for others. Show love to a hurting people in their time of need, and you will never lack for someone to hear your message of salvation.

Compassion Ministering

To be an effective chaplain or minister, you must possess a *real* compassion and love for people. Compassion is an emotion. It cannot simply be turned on and off. An emotion cannot be instantly generated and suddenly be there when it's needed, but there is a way to cause compassion to germinate in your soul. Jesus was touched with compassion[4] for people when they were hungry, sick, or grieving at the death of an only son as was the widow woman. Chaplains, by nature, cannot escape being touched by what they see as they walk among people. Did you catch that? So many are not touched because they do not walk among people that are in desperate need. Jesus's greatest emotions that stirred within Him were over the souls of people.

Once we baptized a woman who had an incurable social disease. We were unaware of her medical condition at the time of her baptism. She received the Holy Ghost while still in the baptismal tank and became a faithful church attendee. About a year later, she called my wife and confided in her that she had this disease, and that the day she was baptized, God had healed her. It has been over twenty years since that phone call, and she is still healed and still active in church. Would this have been the case had she not been shown compassion? The strange thing was that her husband had the same disease, never was converted, and never was healed, but the woman never was re-infected in all their remaining years.

Chaplains and preachers will minister to all kinds of people in the areas that have opened to them. Kindness is the hallmark of the love that God has placed within the minister's heart for others. I was a corporate chaplain for many years and I can remember a lady who had rumors going around the plant where she worked as to her sexual orientation. At first she seemed to stay as far away as possible from me. One day she went into the hospital, and I sent one of my chaplains by to see her. After she recovered and was back at

---

[4] (Matthew 20:34, Mark 1:41)

39

work, she would search me out anytime she knew I was in the plant. She wanted to talk about her life, her daughter, and unburden herself to someone who seemed to care. I believe that because of her lifestyle, she might have thought that I would not care about or minister to her. It was just one kind act that changed all of that.

Depression is one of the many needs that you will have to come to grips with. I put it that way because you may have to take a step back and view life from the other person's vantage point and not from your own experiences and how your life has been lived. A chaplain, as a Christian, naturally has a different vantage point. The very laws of God's kingdom are at work in the chaplain's life, therefore their outlook is more positive and hopeful than that of some others. The very fact that a chaplain has chosen this ministry testifies to this. Being a spiritual and emotional caregiver is a fruit of the second great commandment, to love your neighbor as yourself. These laws are comparable to the laws that God put in nature, like the law of gravity which works unseen and continually. Depressed people, non-Christians, and those who have lost their faith, often do not have the same outlook as those in ministry. Somewhere along the way, they lost their direction, or possibly never found it at all. Chaplains or ministers come alongside and help them find their way.

Recently I was exposed to some very cutting-edge research on depression and the medicine that has been used to treat it since the inception of antidepressants. This research shows there is very little that antidepressants do to help people. In fact, there is quite a lot of evidence that they hurt more than they help since they treat the brain as the cause of depression instead of dealing with what is going on in the person's life. In many cases a placebo worked as well and sometimes better than the antidepressants. How could this be? Could it be that the depressed person felt they were being cared for and that there was hope for them through a magical pill? Let me clarify. Chaplains and ministers are neither doctors or psychologists, nor do we intend to do their work. We would never

40

tell anyone to stop taking their meds as that is not our place. However, the chaplain is there to help people find their way emotionally and spiritually, from our hearts and not from a medical framework. We understand that people have certain emotional needs that the medical field is not able to resolve. Depressed folks need hope, a sense of self-worth, to feel cared for, and someone who will listen to their story. I dare say, everyone needs to be loved.

There is a time when people need mental health assistance and counseling beyond what a chaplain or minister can offer. In those cases, we recommend them for professional care. An example of somewhere this might occur is during a crisis situation such as a natural disaster when chaplains are called upon to give what is called Psychological First-Aid. This is when chaplains are processors in the thick of all the chaos, talking with people and listening to their stories. Hearing their grieving, listening to their fears, and comforting them. During this process we will sometimes come upon those who need further mental health assistance. A chaplain will forward the individual to a mental-health professional.

Depression can come from hopelessness. What of the dead-end job, the sudden "love" rejection, the loss of a job, the death of a companion or close friend? What about an overwhelming situation at work, an unresolved conflict, or an overbearing boss? What if there is sickness or an accident that leaves their life changed and their future in doubt? Come walk with me through the lives of some people I have cared for in the past. Unless you leave your world and walk into their world, you will have no idea what they are going through.

When I wrote most of my notes, our chaplain team covered parts of two states and ten locations. There were approximately three thousand, six hundred fifty (3,650) salary and hourly employees with families at the time. Anyone can quickly see that this was an open door of ministry to many more than the eighty souls I was pastoring at my church.

I assigned other chaplains and myself to make weekly visits to each location. I am inserting the following excerpt from my notes to give the reader insight into what it was like to be a spiritual and emotional caregiver in a corporate environment. This is a typical example of my encounters and thoughts as I walked through a chicken plant this day, available for and seeking the soul in need of my ministry.

As I was Writing this, the Stench was Still in my Nostrils …

My clothes are reeking with a mixture of hot dirty fowls, barnyard off-casting, fresh blood, and wet feathers. I had just passed by a group of men hanging twenty-eight chickens every sixty seconds. Only a red light burns to keep the chickens from jumping off the conveyor belt. There they stand, hour after hour, working as fast as they can, dust and small pieces of feathers floating in the air. The stench is horrid, especially on this hot day. The chickens had to be wet down to keep them from dying. Between the wet fowls and the heat, the smell was horrendous.

Standing on cement for eight to twelve hours a day becomes almost unbearable. Here stand seven souls. I speak to them and they acknowledge that I am there, barely looking up.

Just around the corner an electrical shock is administered to each bird. An automatic blade cuts deep into the back of the chicken's head as it travels hanging upside-down, six inches from the bird in front of it. From this point, there is a pool of blood reaching several hundred feet

…there is a pool of blood reaching several hundred feet.

where the upside-down chickens are bled out, all while traveling down this hanging conveyor line.

Here stands another soul stationed to catch the few fortunate ones that escaped their first planned execution. He has a knife and every few seconds manually ends the life of another chicken. I greet him even though he cannot stop to visit because that line of birds stops for no one. Every three seconds a chicken is passing by. He knows that I am there and that I will be available to talk with him at the next break.

Walking around the corner past the last large pool of coagulating blood, steam rolls out of several machines that loosen and then remove the feathers. The smell of wet chicken feathers is more absorbed into your skin and lungs than smelled.

Finally, this passes into a large, several-thousand square-foot room with hundreds of workers. Here everything is being done to prepare the chickens for the next and final area where they will be cut into pieces and packaged. Every conceivable part of a chicken is seen here; you never have to wonder what each part of a chicken looks like again after being in this room.

Of all the jobs in the world, I believe that this type of meat-processing is some of the most tedious and grueling work there is. Hour after hour, nothing to do but the same one cut, or three snips with the scissors while someone else is placing legs in a package to be sealed.

This is repetitive work, work that does not take much thinking after doing it so many times. Nothing to do but think, think about your problems, think about your low end job, think about how you are going to make ends meet, think about your misery. I look into their faces and into their eyes. What am I looking for?

As I reflect, I realize I am looking for that broken heart, those in deep despair. That one needing a friend... Do you know what it is like to never have a friend? I am looking for the ones who wear the mask but deep inside have trouble loving themselves. Do you know what it is to look into the eyes of a young mother who has lost hope long ago? Pregnant again, already raising three children on her own. Betrayal and rejection are hope-stealers. She is only going through the motions of living now.

43

The eyes tell the story more than the words that are spoken. Have you ever seen the swollen blacked eye and split lip of a lady who was beaten the night before? She still has to go to work or lose her job. Have you looked into her eyes and seen that frightened, hurting little girl that lives on the inside?

What about the supervisor who is working six and sometimes seven days a week? He sometimes works ten to fourteen hours in a day depending on what is happening at the plant that particular week. I once asked a supervisor if he knew where a certain street was in town. He said, "I have lived here for four years and I know the way to work and back home, and I know the way to Wal-Mart."

People everywhere are just trying to keep up with the pace of life and what their jobs demand. Yet they have souls.

Sometimes our Sunday morning, Sunday night and midweek services just do not meet the needs of some people. Can we not minister to them? Did not Christ mandate us to go and walk among them? Jesus walked among the sinners and was their friend too!

Go ye therefore into the highways, and as many as ye shall find, bid to the marriage. So those servants went out into the highways, and gathered together all as many as they found, both bad and good: and the wedding was furnished with guests.
Matthew 22:9-10

To think of the very idea …Jesus was a friend of sinners! He cared for the everyday working person, even the ones who did not have the greatest opportunity to sit in the synagogues. There are thousands and thousands who are outside the walls of our churches that don't seem to find their way to the inside.

I walk into the plant manager's office and speak to him. I know his first name and he knows mine. Not too long ago, if I had passed him on the street, he might not have given me the time of day, but now we are partners. I am there to help carry his load. In our casual conversation I ask him, "Did you know that one of your worker's mother passed away last night?" I give him her name, and he thanks me. I just helped carry part of his load.

I leave the office area and walk to the break room. As I enter, another supervisor recognizes me and says, "Chaplain, will you be here for a while?"

"I'll stay as long as you need me. What do you need?" I ask.

He answers, "I have a lady who needs to speak with you, I'll send her out." In just a few moments a young lady enters and begins to pour out her troubles. "My sister has a terminal illness. She is in the hospital and they say she has only a few weeks to live." I tell her about the healing power of God and offer to go and pray for her sister if the family requests it. Then I pray with her, for God's comfort and help during this time of her need. I pray right there in front of all the people coming in and out of the break room. In just a few minutes she goes back to work.

Next, I put on the same sanitary clothing the other workers have to wear and walk through the blood, the feathers and the midst of souls walking around from station to station, just being there with them. This is called the ministry of presence. Many times when you can do nothing else, just being there is a source of comfort and brings the understanding that someone cares.

My phone rings early one morning. It's the Human Resources Department on the other end telling me there has been a bad wreck. A van-load of workers was on its way to work when something terrible happened. Some of the victims are headed for a hospital two hours away while the rest are in our local hospital. I immediately call my other chaplains to converge on the two different hospitals. The driver is badly injured and grieving. One of the passengers was thrown out through a window and the van rolled on top of her. They were on the way to work and either the tie-rod broke or the tire blew out; they were not sure.

Grieving family members and coworkers begin filling up the ER. I size up the situation and the amount of people now flooding the waiting room area of the Emergency Room. Defusing needs to be my first goal. I must take the situation from chaos to some semblance of order. I will be ministering to those blaming themselves or assigning blame, those who are grieving, and those in shock, all of whom must be calmed. This might include anything from separating the driver from the other victims and families to taking family members in to view the deceased. So we began by allowing the plant officials to come and show their care and concern but not having them stay until all was resolved. This is how I attend to the concerns of the company and care for the ones who were hurt. I leave in the wee hours of the morning after the last one has either been released or placed in their hospital room.

Arriving at another plant later in the week, I greet several workers one at a time as I walk through the plant. I approach a group of three men and greet them. They introduce themselves and then go back to their discussion. I decide to go on to another area presuming there is not much immediate need at that work station. I walk down a set of stairs and looking over my shoulder, I see that someone is following me. It is one of the men from the work station I had just left. Out of sight of the other workers he says, "I am having problems in my marriage. Can you talk with my wife and me?" I arrange a time when we can meet.

On another visit I speak with a man who says, "Can you counsel with my teenager? He is having problems with drugs again." Later I walk into a lunchroom and someone else confides that his family situation is floundering. I listen for ten minutes letting him unburden. I will go by and check on him often for the next few weeks. I am reminded of what the Lord said about the Good Samaritan:

> *But a certain Samaritan, as he journeyed, came where he was:*
> *and when he saw him, he had compassion [on him],*
> *And went to [him], and bound up his wounds ...*
> **Luke 10:33-34**

You have to come close to see them, and when you get near people, you will gain something called compassion. It is an emotion that our Lord had: ...*when he saw the multitudes, he was moved with compassion on them...* (Matthew 9:36) Compassion will move you into action. My heart goes out to each and every one waiting for a Samaritan to come by.

Can you hear that? It's Jesus calling. "I need help, I have problems, my marriage is going for broke." You say Jesus never was married so it can't be Him calling. You think not? Listen again ...

I was an hungred, and ye gave me meat:...Naked, and ye clothed me...I was sick, and ye visited me...I was in prison, and ye came ...
Matthew 25:35-36

I'm Jesus from *Let Me Tell You a Story* by Tony Campolo

"During World War II, the Nazis came into a Polish village, rounded up the Jews, lined them up in front of a firing squad, and killed them. The bodies of the dead fell into a huge grave that the Jews themselves had dug.

As dirt was shoveled over the bodies, no one was aware there was a boy being buried among the dead who had not been touched by any of the bullets. He slowly dug his way out of the grave.

By the time he emerged from the dirt, night had fallen. The boy ran back into the village, hoping some of the people there would take him in. But every door that opened was immediately shut when the people inside saw who he was. They recognized the boy. They knew he was one of the Jews who had been shot at by the firing squad. They wanted nothing to do with him, lest the Nazis punish them for harboring a Jewish child. Finally, he knocked on one door, and before it could be shut in his face, he cried out to the woman inside, "Don't you recognize me? I'm Jesus! Don't you recognize me? The woman swept the child into the house, and from that day on

> Don't you recognize me? I'm Jesus!

47

cared for him as though he was one of her own.

In later life, when that boy had grown up, he always remembered that fateful evening, but he could never figure out why he had said what he said."[5]

Shall we ask Jesus when did we see you with these kinds of needs? He will answer,

> ...Inasmuch as ye have done [it] unto... the least of these
> my brethren, you did [it] unto me.
> **Matthew 25:40**

Why did the boy shout, "I am Jesus, don't you recognize me?" Could it be that it was really Jesus doing the speaking? Can you hear him calling to you today?

- "I am Jesus ... my marriage is on the rocks."
- "I haven't slept in several days."
- "I am dying on the inside... will you help me?"
- "My wife left me and I don't know what to do."
- "I have an alcohol habit and it is destroying my life."
- "I have cancer ... I am sick. Will you visit me?"
- "My child is in jail ... will you go see him?"

Compassion in Illness and Suffering

(Hopefully you will realize compassion, maybe even garner a tear, by the time you finish this chapter.)

My mind had drifted a bit while listening to the sermon. I was suddenly jolted back into the setting I was sharing with a hundred or so church members, just in time to hear these words, "If you can listen to this without tears in your eyes something is wrong with you." What was he talking about, and why were my emotions in question? Ah yes, he was preaching on the subject of the beating and death of our Savior and how terrible it was. Why was I feeling like I had missed something?

---

[5] Tony Campolo, *Let Me Tell You a Story,* (Nashville, TN: Thomas Nelson, 2000) 26-27

As the speaker finished his sermon, he was trying to lead us into the direction of a particular emotional response. What should I do now? I checked my emotions and found to my dismay I did not have tears in my eyes as the minister indicated I should. So what was wrong with me? Perhaps I am different than everyone else on the face of the earth, but I do not find that I can muster up emotions that are just not there. Should I be ashamed that I did not have the right emotions about such a horrible event as the crucifixion of Jesus? I am sure that I have heard that sermon subject preached a thousand times before, and at times I am sure genuine, sorrowful emotions were there. I understand that there are actors who can cry at will, but I feel it would be false if I did it, not that I could. So what was wrong with me? No, the question is, what was wrong with the speaker? How did he depart from his message to impose his expected emotional response on the audience? Perhaps he honestly felt the intenseness of his message and mistakenly believed that everyone should be on the same page, at the same moment.

Here is a great lesson for the chaplain or minister. Never presume to know what someone else is going through or how they are feeling. Never demand emotions or actions according to your own thinking of what they should be feeling or doing. If you make that a rule in your ministry, it will save you from many errors of assumption and help you avoid damage that may be done when you are trying to care for someone.

I have never had to deal with great excruciating and prolonged pain so there is no way I can know what someone else is going through who is suffering from that kind of pain. An elder teacher who I greatly admire told of a suffering woman who he went to visit regularly. One day he went to her house, and during the normal course of conversation, he asked how her day was going. She replied, "Oh, it is a good day; today, I have not had pain for an hour." Just hearing that stuns me. I cannot conceive twenty-three hours of pain and only one hour without pain and call that a good day. As a chaplain, I need to let the person talking to me tell me what they are going through. How are they feeling? Are they

49

discouraged, in much pain, lonely, missing a departed spouse? Or perhaps they are feeling better, looking forward to going home, feeling positive or even upbeat.

I should also not presume to think that even if I have had a similar experience as the individual who is speaking to me that I will know what they are going through. Each person's suffering, whether physical or emotional, is unique. Because I lost my older sister does not mean I know what someone else is going through who has just lost their child. My sister died before I was born and all I ever knew of her were the stories I had heard, but I had no relationship with her. My situation is entirely different from someone who has just lost their family member with whom they had a close relationship. Even in a family of five siblings there can be different relationships which will bring different levels of grieving.

I can remember being called by the social worker of a certain hospital to help with a family struggle. The time had come, and the children were wrestling with a decision to pull their father off of life support. Two of the siblings had made the decision that it was time. One of the siblings was adamantly against it. Why the strong difference in feelings? After talking for a while, it was uncovered that the sibling who was resistant was the one who had a very broken relationship with his father. Alcohol had been a problem and he had moved several hundred miles away. Being estranged and not in a good relationship with his father was causing him to oppose the rest of the family, even though the best decision for them and the father was to let him pass in peace.

People will react with different feelings to similar situations depending on the background and circumstances an individual brings to a situation. Someone who has watched their mother go through cancer and die, then later finds out they have stage-one cancer, may not be positive about their prognosis because of their prior familial experience compared to the emotions of someone in the same situation who knows a cancer survivor. Past experiences and relationships cause people to react differently while going through the same kinds of struggles. Being a good listener is the key. In another chapter we will share more on the art of listening.

Next, don't presume to tell anyone how they should feel. Remember, every person reacts differently to situations depending on the path of life they have traveled. I knew a man who was a great minister and speaker and could talk to thousands at a time, yet when it came to a one-on-one conversation with someone, he was completely uncomfortable. It was my great honor to be the one to take him to the airport after a meeting. The trip lasted two hours, and the whole time I talked and asked questions, not knowing I was making him want to get away from me. I offered to follow him into the airport and wait with him while he waited for his plane, while he tried to dissuade me. I did not grasp what was happening, nor did I read his body language. So, I followed him into the airport, trying to be nice while desiring to pick his brain about his great knowledge. It was only later that I found out he had suffered extreme rejection in his life which made him very uncomfortable in one-on-one interactions. This is a unique type of case in which there is not much room to minister since emotional and spiritual caregiving is mostly conducted one-on-one. Perhaps what should have happened is that I should have noticed by his reactions to my questions that he was trying to tell me to back off and build a better bridge that would show him I would not reject him and that he could trust me. Only then would I have stood a chance of ministering to him.

I have seen some people that can stand a lot of physical pain, while others are propelled into tears with very little pain. Even living with someone you see every day, you still don't necessarily know what they are suffering. My own mother, with machines making her breathe every breath every day of her life, serves as an example. Knowing that a simple, prolonged power-outage could claim her life might cause fear and doubt to plague the heart. So what is the answer? Listen. You have to be a listener. Let them tell you.

Chaplains are not counselors per se, although they do counsel. They are emotional and spiritual caregivers. They are not problem-fixers for people, but they will walk through the valleys of life with them. Sometimes, caregiving is a ministry of presence and a listening ear. I have been married for forty-five years, and it took me some time, but I have learned that when my wife wants to talk about a problem in her world, she does not want me to fix the problem; she wants me to listen. She is unburdening herself and needs a listener and someone to care.

Some pain is physical and some is emotional, especially when linked to certain memories. There came a call to a certain agency one day from a woman who said she was pregnant and wanted to give her child up for adoption. When following up on that call, the agency investigated as was their common practice. Some startling facts were discovered. The woman was not pregnant, and she was married with two children. What caused this woman to call the agency, wanting to give up a non-existent child? She was in pain, emotional pain. She had had an abortion many years before and her mind was trying to undo the pain and guilt she felt by reliving the pregnancy. This time she would make the right decision and give up her child for adoption. This was a cycle she had gone through several times. There are times when a chaplain must recognize and realize that they are not equipped to deal with some things and situations and must pass them on to a mental-health professional who specializes in the area where help is needed. While I know that abortion is a very difficult subject with so many strong feelings attached, the scope of this book is not one of condemnation but rather one of caring. My thoughts on the subject cannot and should not change the caring and emotional support that I give to the person in need.

Jesus came not to condemn the world, but that through Him this fallen world might be saved. Jesus did not condemn the woman at the well, the thief on the cross, or King David, but forgave them. What a wonderful thing it is when a caregiver helps a burden-laden soul lay down their load. No wonder the angels in heaven rejoice over one sinner who repents.

Chaplains are much like the Good Samaritan who found the man beaten, robbed and left half-dead, a man who did not choose to be beaten and left to die. The man might have chosen the path that led him to the robbers, but he did not choose to be robbed. The Good Samaritan saw him and helped him. He had compassion on him and began to bind up his wounds, ministering to him. The Good Samaritan paid the whole price to get the man nursed back to health, and said he would pay even more if there was any other cost incurred. Now we are the Good Samaritans in the place of Jesus Christ on this earth, and it is our ministry to find those who have been beat up by sin, mistakes, or even the chance that happens to all. The single mother who many times did not choose to be single, the fatherless, the poor and the destitute. All of these have some combination of fear, guilt, sins, mistakes, shame and chance that has taken them to the place where you find them.

This reminds me of another story by Tony Campolo in his book, *Let Me Tell You a Story*.[6] It is a true story about Tony himself. I will tell it in my own words to shorten it some. Tony had flown to Hawaii and had a case of jetlag. About midnight he was done sleeping and a bit hungry, so he left his hotel in search of a cup of coffee and some donuts. He found a small diner that some might refer to as a "greasy spoon." As he entered, he saw a counter with swivel stools, and since no one else was in the diner, he sat on a middle stool. An old man with a dirty apron asked what he wanted. "Donuts and coffee would be fine," he replied, so the old man slid him a cup of coffee and retrieved for him a couple of donuts from under a glass cover.

While Tony was sitting there, the door burst open, and a group of prostitutes came in, loud and appearing to be somewhat drunk. They filled the stools on each side of Tony. One of them named Agnes, looked at the calendar and simply said that the next day was

---

[6] Tony Campolo, *Let Me Tell You a Story*, (Nashville, TN: Thomas Nelson, 2000) 216-219

her birthday. One of the other women said, "Why are you telling us Agnes? You don't expect us to give you a birthday party do you?"

Agnes said, "No, I have never had a birthday party."

After the women finished eating and left, Tony asked the man behind the counter, "Do they come in here every night?"

> No, I have never had a birthday party.

"Yes. What do you want to know fer?"

Tony went on, "Does Agnes come in here every night?"

"Yes. What do you want to know fer?"

"Well," Tony said, "I heard that tomorrow is Agnes's birthday, and I thought it would be nice to give her a party. I will make ready the decorations, and we can surprise her."

"Yeah. That will fix old Agnes. I will bake a cake for her," said the old man with the dirty apron. So it was, and so they did, and then the women came. Loud and somewhat drunken again, they came stumbling into the diner after their night of work. Partway across the room Agnes stopped as she read, "Happy Birthday Agnes." The old man came rushing out with the birthday cake. "Hey, cut the cake, Agnes! We all want a piece," he said.

Agnes just looked at it and finally she said, "I have never had a birthday cake. Would you mind if I just took it home? So Agnes left with the cake, and the other women just stood there watching the door as she went out.

After Agnes left, Tony ran up to them and grabbing their hands he said, "Let me pray for you." So right there at about three in the morning, Tony prayed for Agnes and the other women, for God to help them.

When they all left, the old man with a dirty apron asked, "What kind of church do you go to?"

Tony said, "I go to the kind of church that gives birthday parties for prostitutes at three in the morning."

The old man with the dirty apron said, "No, you don't. There is no church like that, cause if there was, I would join it."

I wonder if that is the kind of church that the Good Samaritan went to? You never know what someone has been through in life or why they are the way they are. Take yourself out of the nice setting where you might have been raised and step into the shoes of Agnes. What brought about the fact that no one cared enough to ever give a little girl growing up a birthday party? Who was not there for her and how was she raised? Was she shipped from foster home to foster home? Did she live in a dysfunctional and abusive home? You don't know, nor do I, but our responsibility is just to care and share the love of God.

Being a Starter

There are so many things that are and sound so wonderful and compelling of which I have written just a few, however, there are many days, weeks and months when no one seems to share your vision or want to help in jail ministry or any other ministry. I have found that many people cannot or will not jump on board until the cart is already rolling. Many times that leaves one or two people with vision, burden, and guts to get it started. No matter what your ministry goal is, someone has to be the starter. You could become discouraged, angry, or even bitter, but remember to thank God for your unique talent of being a starter. Not everyone has this talent or faith to do what you do. Remember the people God has placed within your hands. I remember one time we were involved in an alcohol and drug training program based out of our church. Having a drug and alcohol or anger management training program is a great way to get your foot in the door with a local jail and/or probation department. It's a starting point.

Faithfulness to something once it is started takes commitment. I remember that our church team had become discouraged and went to the Senior Pastor asking for a meeting to vote about shutting down the program. In prayer, God spoke to me and said, "Go buy some H.M.O. figurines and tell them these represent the people I have placed within their hands." H.M.O. stands for Hand Made Object, which are per scale copies of people and other things. After everything had been said, and the vote to disband was apparent, they finally let me speak. I gave each of them a handful of the little figurines and told them what God had said. Tears flowed and burdens were rekindled. Consequently, the program continued. There will be days like these, but keep moving if you want to see where God is going. Finish what has been started.

I will preface this by saying that chaplains will run into many questions from people during the trials of their lives. They will cry out just like Job did, needing answers. To some questions there are no answers that can be offered to satisfy the tormented soul.

Chaplains must never become Job's comforters; neither can they afford to be the responders to every situation or provider of answers for every question. However, there are some questions that necessitate having some type of an answer. I refer to these as directional answers. While these answers may not bring resolution to the whole question, they can point the struggling person in a direction that can bring them comfort and a measure of peace.

I first discovered that I did not have all the answers when I was far less trained as an emotional and spiritual caregiver. In fact, I had no idea what to say or how to answer the question, "Why me God?"

It was somewhere in the middle of the night that a call came from the hospital. "Chaplain you are needed in the nursery." Rushing to the unit, I found a large group of nurses and doctors gathered around in a half-circle near the door. Inside the room, about half-way toward the far wall, was a lone figure in a rocking chair with her back to me. She was cradling her baby in her arms. She was crying out very loudly to God for an answer. She was pleading her case directly to God. "Why me God? I never drank, or took drugs … why me God?" Over and over she cried out. I

> Why me God? I never drank, or took drugs...why me God?

later found out that her baby had been born with severe deformities and had lived just two dozen days. The baby was now dead, and as she clutched the precious little body, she continued to cry out for an answer. No one would take the dead body from this grieving mother until she was ready to surrender her lost baby, so they had called the chaplain.

What was I to do? At a total loss on how to help, and being untrained on how to intervene, I did the only thing I knew to do...I prayed. My prayer was desperate, "God, you have to help me!" It seemed like a half-hour passed before God helped me, but I am sure it must have only been a few minutes. I heard an inner voice say "Go, lay your hand on her shoulder and say it is okay. You do not have to understand right now." Immediately, I felt like this would never work, but having nothing else to go on, and struggling within myself for a few minutes, I walked across the room and laid my hand on her right shoulder and said, "It is okay. You don't have to understand right now." Immediately she stopped crying out, and silence filled the room for several minutes. Those were long minutes as I stood there knowing that all eyes were focused on my back. I could think of nothing else to offer. To say a prayer did not seem to fit at that moment. No verses of scripture came to my mind that might answer her cry. Then slowly she wrapped up that little body, stood, and handed her baby back to the nurse. Then she left. I had no idea what I had done, but it had worked.

Later, through study about these kinds of situations, I discovered that this young mother was not given the answer for which she was desperately crying, but what she did receive was permission not to understand. This is an example of a directional answer. The question was never answered, but rather, the direction gave her the release from having to understand, "Why me God?" at that moment.

While the spiritual caregiver may not have a satisfactory answer for the hurting soul, they can be a comforter, provide a ministry of presence, and at the right time, offer a directional answer that can point the suffering person in a direction that will help them find peace. It must be understood that every situation is unique, and every person's reaction can or will be different, so a one-size-fits-all answer will never suffice. With all the training you can gain, you still need the guidance of God. Chaplains that have more training than you, years of experience, and are of good report are a great benefit as well. Our chaplain mentors will be glad to work with you in any way that we can when you come to a situation where you need some advice.

A Man Named Sidney

Today there are ever increasing numbers of homeless people. There are many reasons why they are there, from the mentally ill to those who have just given up and have chosen homelessness as a means to exist. The sadness of life seems to surround them like a blanket. Being near them knowing they have been wearing the same clothes for months on end without washing them or themselves is just one of the drawbacks when ministering to them. Living in the South where it is very hot and humid can make it challenging because the smell of body odor and urine is almost unbearable.

Alcohol and drug abuse are rampant as is their doing anything to get that next fix or bit of money to buy more alcohol or drugs. My heart goes out to the young women who have lost all pretenses of sexual limitations. Living hand to mouth, anything goes, and all that is important is the next high. Down, down goes their self-respect and self-worth. Now they are only living for the substance that helps them forget.

It was a hot summer day at the fairgrounds when I first saw one of our city's homeless. He was passed out drunk, lying at an odd angle, under one of the tents. There was a group of young boys poking at him with a stick and making fun of him.

I didn't think much about it, oh, but maybe a momentary feeling sorry for him, but life goes on. Then that winter, on a very cold day, I had gone to church a bit early and was down at the altar praying before service was to begin. It was a bitter cold day, and the church was nice and warm. A doctor friend of mine was teaching a series on the family, and I was really looking forward to hearing him speak this particular morning. As I was praying, I thought my mind had drifted and a conversation was running through my brain. It went like this: "It's sure cold outside today; and I said, "It sure is warm in here." Both of these statements I thought were my own thoughts, but then I came to the realization that it was a conversation between God and me. It was God who had said, "It's sure cold outside today." And it was me that said, "It sure is warm in here." The reason I know it was God was because of the next words He said, "There are some people who slept outside last night." Immediately my mind went to the man I saw passed out in the summer. I knew that God was concerned about the homeless in our city.

I procured a bottle of coffee and some week-old loaves of bread that had been donated to the children's home where I was working. We did not have resources to also help the homeless. I went to the fairgrounds and started looking for the homeless. The first person I came upon was Sidney. After giving him the bread and coffee, I asked him if he could get a group of the homeless together on the next Sunday morning telling him I would bring them breakfast. Sure enough, the next Sunday Sidney and a half-dozen others were there, and so our homeless ministry began.

Eventually, we took one of our old school buses and used it as a

> ...we took one of our old school buses and used it as a makeshift church.

makeshift church. We would drive it down to the fairgrounds, park it in the alley nearest the fence, and wait until they came to eat and hear the Word of God. Many times I would have to prod them out of the hiding places where they slept. Filth and human waste littered these places continually. And yet, God was concerned about these who seemed to be on the loosest rungs of life's ladder.

As I got to know them and brought as many of them as I could to church, I began to hear their stories. Sidney had been a soldier. Somewhere along life's road, he had gotten into a fight with another man, and the man had died as a result of injuries sustained during the fight, and Sidney had gone to prison. After Sidney paid his debt to society and came back to our city, things were not the same. Being knocked down rung after rung, he ended up on the streets. I knew that Sidney struggled with not being able to forgive himself for the man's death.

Ultimately, we rented a small building and began to hold services there. We sang and preached each week, and of course, we fed them. Some got baptized and received the Holy Ghost. On

Thanksgiving Day, the whole church went and fed them all a full turkey dinner and sat down and ate with them. Most of the homeless in our city were able to get off the streets one way or another as a result of our ministering to them. The gospel is like a river of life; wherever it goes, it heals the land.

Two homeless people stand out to me. One was a young man who had gotten baptized and attended church, yet somehow he just could not shake loose of his old lifestyle and went to prison for killing a man. The other was Sidney. I can remember him walking along peering in through windows in town. He would go by the barbershop and look in. Our barber was a Spirit-filled man and would always give him something to eat. Somehow, Sidney seemed trapped in his world and died sometime after I left town. I hope and pray that something he heard during those services led him to salvation. I only regret that I could not have done more for Sidney, but of this I am sure, God cared about Sidney.

As a minster or a chaplain, God may ask you to do things that you may not like or want to do. For example, go someplace that is not a nice church building with all cleaned-up people. A real love for people is the most important thing you can have because it is a heart like unto Christ's own.

The Epicurean Dilemma
God is good, yet there is suffering

As a chaplain or a minister, you will encounter many questions. Indeed, you will have quandaries of your own to resolve before you can help others. This is one you will encounter.

The title of this chapter does not give the whole of the Epicurean Dilemma but condenses it down to "God is good, yet there is suffering." This dilemma points an accusing finger at God as either not all powerful, evil with mean dark motives, or He is no God at all, for if He was God then there would be no evil.

Let's talk opposites for a moment. If there were no evil, how would we know good? One cannot know what immoral is unless we have a moral law-giver. Ravi Zacharias, famous author and apologist, defends the Christian faith in public settings everywhere. Former atheist turned Christian, he teaches and lectures about the high moral authority of God and His existence in the universe and in the lives of men. When challenged that there was not such a thing as evil, therefore there was not a God, Ravi puts it this way in his book, *Can Man Live Without God?* "If there is such a thing as evil, aren't you assuming there is such a thing as good?" "If there is such a thing as good," I countered, "you must affirm a moral law on the basis of which to differentiate between good and evil." [7]

Some stumble over not wanting to believe there is a God, who is a moral authority, and others try to reason away God and His moral authority. Such were the Epicureans and their thought-up dilemma.

While taking more chaplains' training, we were assigned to write on different topics. The rules stated that we had to write about ourselves and a subject from a list provided. This chapter is on one of the topics I chose, The Epicurean Dilemma: God is good, yet there is suffering.

---

[7] Ravi Zacharias, *Can Man Live Without God?*, (Nashville, Tennessee, W Publishing Group, a division of Thomas Nelson, Inc., 1994) 182

The following arguments are what I selected to address in connection with my topic of choice.

- Is God willing to prevent evil, but not able? Then he is not omnipotent.
- Is He able, but not willing? Then He is malevolent.
- Is He both able and willing? Then whence cometh evil?
- Is He neither able nor willing? Then why call him God?

I have included a copy of the entire dilemma as written by a follower of Epicurus, at the end of this chapter.

Some people have honest questions that cry for an answer. Still others are looking to either blame God or eliminate Him from the equation, thereby relieving themselves of the responsibility of obedience to Him.

As a little boy on the Philippine Islands, my father was asked a question. He had traveled to bring the gospel to yet another remote village. The elders of that village asked him, "Is your God all-powerful so that He can do anything and create anything?"

My father's answer was, "Yes, God is all powerful." (Omnipotent)

The villagers next asked, "Then, can your God create a stone too large for Him to pick up?" This is a trick question created to trap a person who believes in God or an attempt to relieve the asker's own conscience from the knowledge of God. Most times this is not an honest-hearted question.

There are haunting questions in each of our hearts with which we struggle, mine included. I am not blind or deaf. God has given me a mind that is at least aware of the world around me and its happenings. With today's access to world information, we not only face our own questions but the questions brought about by the dilemmas of a whole world. So the questions roll in like the tide on the seashore, seemingly never-ending, because evil, godless, depraved events seem to be endless. The sea erodes the very land on which we live; likewise, these quandaries erode the very pillars

63

supporting life and faith. Even good unanswered questions can erode a person's faith as the waves of dilemma come crashing onto the shores of one's life.

I have wondered at war. I have wondered at tragic events. Each time an innocent life is snuffed out, or a young child is abused, neglected, or murdered, I wonder, where is God?

My heart was torn asunder when I visited the Holocaust Museum in Washington D. C. as I found myself unable to fathom how one person could administer such atrocities on other people who were also created by God. So the question came crashing into my soul, where were you God when these things were happening?

In my own life, the "Why?" question

...God healed my father but allowed my other to die a horrible suffering death.

---

haunted me for eleven long years. I could not understand why God healed my father but allowed my mother to die a horrible suffering death. In other words, I knew God could heal because He had healed my father, but when it came to my mother, He did not. This brought confusion and resentment into my life that grew into hatred. I wandered in the wilderness, alienated from my faith in God. The wilderness is where eroding unanswered questions eat away at your core, if you let them. It does not matter if your questions are honest concerns. Without God there is only "outside of God." What I am trying to say is that without faith and hope in a just and perfect God, there is only faith and hope in the goodness of godless humans with their arrogant, logical, and educated answers to the cruelties and perversions of mankind, which is no hope at all. That alone is rational explanation enough to realize it is God we trust for the answers to the questions, yet in times of deep crisis, it is irrational thinking that comes to the surface.

Personal tragedy in my life at a young age led to my own "why" questioning. I knew God could do anything. So why doesn't He when He can? This classic example of my belief in what God should do, which was not fulfilled according to my expectation, led to misunderstanding, confusion, and eventual bitterness.

The "Why?" Question

If God is so powerful and good, why is there evil disease and cruel sufferings? Where is the great God who will come and save us and destroy the evil? As a teenager, the waves of questioning and doubt started crashing on the shore of my life, sweeping away my trust and belief like a tsunami that uproots and takes everything back out to the sea to be buried in its dark depths. Buried in the depths is the place I was for eleven long years.

Could God have prevented that evil disease that attacked my mother? Could He have come and rescued her after the attack and healed her? The answer is *Yes!* God could have, but the reality is that He did not. So is God malevolent? Is He enjoying the suffering and grief people go through? Is there some evil dark side to God? These are real questions haunting and lurking on the edges of the mind, eroding the pillars of the heart. He could have, but He did not ...Why God?

I did not miss the second line of the dilemma: "Is God able?" Yes, He is able, but *is* He willing? The first part of that statement takes care of itself if you are a believer. So the question becomes, "Is He willing?" My answer to this question is, *at times.* Sometimes God prevents evil; sometimes He allows evil to run its course. If you don't believe that, perhaps you might ask a man named Job. God had a hedge around Job but took it down.

While pastoring in a little mountain town in Washington state, way up in the mountains on U.S. Route twelve, a narrow two-lane road that some have designated the second deadliest road in America, God did prevent evil. I was a bi-vocational pastor and worked about ten miles up this two-lane road, with the mountains on one side and a cliff on the other. My wife and children drove up to bring my lunch, and as they were returning, had God not intervened, I might have never seen them alive again. Traveling back down the winding narrow mountainous road, my wife said that God spoke to her and said, "Pull over." Now on most places along that road there are no shoulders and only guardrails to keep cars from being pushed over the cliff, so there would normally be no place to pull over even if she wanted to. At that very moment, there was a break between the next set of guardrails, so she pulled over. It was just before a corner, and there was only enough room to get our little compact car off the road. Suddenly, two log trucks came racing around the corner, one on each side of the road. My whole family would have been pushed over the cliff, no doubt on a quick trip to eternity, but God stopped the evil that day. Yet everyday there are wrecks which take innocent lives and cause countless sufferings. So why does God prevent one accident and allow another?

> My whole family would have been pushed over the cliff.

With questions like this, I had to come to the place where I simply trusted God. Now, I trust that God is good and there is no malevolence in Him. He is just and knows things too hard for me to understand. Nature teaches about God, and that everything is His handiwork. I know the sun is good and needful for life. I enjoy the sun, and it helps plants and trees grow, but I do not know how it affects the earth's winds or keeps from burning itself out. I do not even understand what some learned men know about the sun, but I do not worry that the sun will not come up tomorrow. I know that it will. I do not have to know everything about God's creation to reap its benefits. Similarly, I do not have to understand how God is dealing with evil; I just know that He is.

I am reminded of the story Corrie ten Boom told about a trip she made with her father when she was a small girl. He was a watchmaker and he had to go into the big city to buy parts. He allowed her to go with him. What wonders she saw that day and then she heard what a little girl did not need to know until later in life. She asked her father about it. Her father asked her to carry his heavy suitcase off the train. She, of course, could not do it and said to her father, "It is too heavy for me to pick up." To this her wise father said, "Yes, and it would be a pretty poor father who would ask his little girl to carry such a load. It's the same way, Corrie, with knowledge. Some knowledge is too heavy for children. When you are older and stronger you can bear it. For now, you must trust me to carry it for you." [8]

I do not understand why God does not stop evil every time or why He allows sickness, disease, death, suffering and sorrow. I do not understand why there are wars, murders and abortion. I cannot understand why neighbors kill neighbors or why evil rulers are left to rule. I have no answers for suffering, tears, divorces and starvation. I cannot understand why teenage boys would kill their own classmates and then kill themselves, nor can I understand suicide bombers.

I have come to a conclusion with a scripture in mind.

Lord, my heart is not haughty, nor mine eyes lofty: neither do I exercise myself in great matters, or in things too high for me.
Psalms 131:1

Some things are just too high for me to understand now but not too high for me to believe that God is in control. He is all-powerful, good, just, and will always do the right thing. I choose to believe that.

When ministering to a suffering or grieving person you will not be able to answer the many unanswerable questions, but you can point them in the direction of not having to understand everything right now and trusting that God is always just. Remember many questions are not being asked for you to answer, but rather it is the tears of the crying soul. Let people express their pain, for in so doing there is release and cleansing, a purging of the emotions. The greatest listeners are many times the greatest caregivers.

---

[8] Corrie ten Boom, John L Scherrill and Elizabeth Scherrill, *The Hiding Place*, (New York, NY, Bantam Books, 1984) 26-27

Epicurean Dilemma Explained

Epicureanism is a system of philosophy based upon the teachings of the ancient Greek philosopher Epicurus, founded around 307 BC. Lactantius, De Lra Deorm was a follower of Epicurus.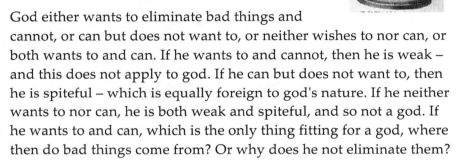

The Riddle of Epicurus, or Problem of Evil, is a famous argument against the existence of an all-powerful and providential God or gods. As recorded by Lactantius:

God either wants to eliminate bad things and cannot, or can but does not want to, or neither wishes to nor can, or both wants to and can. If he wants to and cannot, then he is weak – and this does not apply to god. If he can but does not want to, then he is spiteful – which is equally foreign to god's nature. If he neither wants to nor can, he is both weak and spiteful, and so not a god. If he wants to and can, which is the only thing fitting for a god, where then do bad things come from? Or why does he not eliminate them?

"EPICURUS's old questions are yet unanswered. Is he willing to prevent evil, but not able? then is he impotent. Is he able, but not willing? then is he malevolent. Is he both able and willing? whence then is evil?" [9]

[9] David Hume, *Dialogues Concerning Natural Religion*, (London) 186
Lactantius, De Ira Deorum, 13.19 Eoucyrys, Frag.

It's Not Fair

What is fair? There are many different meanings for fair. It is a *fair* day. She is a *fair*-skinned girl. Other meanings include not excessive or extreme. The performance was *fair*. Baseball even gets in the mix. It is a *fair* ball. There are so many ways to use this word, but when someone says, "It's not *fair*," most people know that the person speaking is revealing that they feel somebody has taken an unfair advantage of them. Most likely, everyone has seen or been a victim of unfairness at some point in their lives.

We hear it often. We see it played out in our daily lives and in the news repeatedly. Someone feels they have been slighted or that someone has treated them unfairly. The truth is everyone has most likely been slighted or done wrong in some way. The shocking fact is this - life is not fair.

If life were fair everything would grind to a halt. It is not fair that as a kid, I was the last one to be picked for a side in the ball-game. I always hated it when no one wanted me on their team. I was not a very good player, and other kids were either more popular or better players than me. It hurt then and probably would now in a similar, but adult scenario. If life were fair, we all would have been picked first. That is absurd and would never work. Can you imagine all the kids standing around waiting to be picked so the game can start? One of the two captains would yell, "All of you are picked first and you are on my team." What about the other poor captain, and hey, who says they should be a captain anyway? To be fair we should all be captains but then where would be the team? What a mess life would be if everything was fair.

I am not advocating unfairness to anyone, nor do I think there ought to be some people with everything while there are other people with nothing. I also believe that we should help anyone in an unfair situation of life when we can. Life, however, is not fair, nor was it meant to be.

For ye have the poor with you always, and whensoever ye will
ye may do them good: but me ye have not always.
Mark 14:7

Life is a combination of time, places, people and events, all to which we must respond. It's about *how* we respond. To quote Craig Nakken in his book, *The Addictive Personality*, "At times in our lives, most of us find this wholeness of peace and beauty, but then it slips away, only to return another time. When it leaves us, we feel sadness and even a slight sense of mourning. This is one of the natural cycles of life, and it is not a cycle we can control. To some extent, we can help these cycles, but for the most part they're uncontrollable. Addiction can be viewed as an attempt to control these uncontrollable cycles. When addicts use a particular object, such as a substance or an event to produce a desired mood change, they believe they can control these cycles."[10]

When we feel that something is not fair, what happens? Does our mood change? Most generally, to some degree or another, it does. Do we become uncomfortable or uneasy, which is an unpleasant feeling? This is natural, but how we deal with it is important. If we could right every wrong and make every unequal situation equal, would not the results be the same as the addict who wants to shield himself or herself from the downward cycles that are altering every mood? The way that addiction is connected to life not being fair is what we do with the resulting emotions when subjected to unfairness and understanding that sometimes we are not treated fairly. What we do with these emotions and facts can lead to an addiction.

Facing up to Life's Unfairness

Life is full of unpleasantness and unfairness. I stated it this way because I have never found unfairness to be pleasant. I learned this early in life, and if I could have done something about it, I would have. What was the source of my unpleasant unfairness? My

---

[10] Craig Nakken, *The Addictive Personality,* (Center City, MN, Hazelden Publishers, 1986) 7

mother took me to a mean man just to let him hurt me. Now you would think that a loving mother would not do something like this but she did. It seemed like she felt it was her duty. Oh, who was this mean man? He is called a dentist. I know if this qualifies as a "that's not fair" in your book, but it sure was in mine at seven-years-old. So we see there are many things in life that are unfair, uncomfortable, and unpleasant, nevertheless, they can be helpful to our growth, and in my case, it probably saved my life (I had terrible abscesses). What is unfair to one person may not be unfair to someone else. Being treated unfairly can leave deep scars on people's lives that last for years.

> My mother took me to a mean man just to let him hurt me.

Failures in life are one of the things that seem full of unfairness. We had a great president who failed miserably many times. He failed in business. He had a nervous breakdown. Twice he failed running for the Senate, was rejected for land officer, and later was defeated for the nomination of Vice-President. He then became President of the United States, only to be assassinated before leaving office. I am not sure how to frame Abraham Lincoln's life, but unfair comes to mind. However, we don't think so much about the unfairness of his life as we do his successes in leading the country through troubled times, enabling poor people through the Homestead Act to obtain land, establishing our national banking system, and standing against enslaving other men.

The point is this, life has its ups and downs. That is what makes life what it is. A wise man, in fact, the wisest man, Solomon, said, *"Time and chance happeneth to them all,"* (Ecclesiastes 9:11). I believe time happens to all and chance happens to everyone but not fairly or equally; they just happen.

On a cold icy day, a young pastor's wife and children decided to go to the mall. During their trip, someone hit them from behind and pushed them in front of an oncoming semi-truck. It was a horrible accident in which the wife and son were killed. The pastor's daughter was rescued by a bystander who pulled her from the burning wreckage. You might say, "It's not fair," that this should happen to someone just going to the mall, minding their own business. And you would be right. That should never happen to anyone. But, if life was fair, and that happened to them, what about the rest of us? To be fair, would not all of us need to have the same life-wrenching experience happen to our family? And to further be fair, why just the mother and the son?

No, life was never meant to be fair, and will never work fairly, but life was meant to be workable. Life has its cycles and its events. The sooner people realize the truth, that life is not fair, it will set them free from the kind of thinking that holds them back emotionally. Feeling sorry for yourself, perceiving that you are being slighted by life, or thinking the cards are stacked against you will drain away your desire to overcome. This in turn will cause you to stagnate.

Everyone has been treated badly and treated others badly at some time or another. As you read this chapter, let those unfair situations surface. Too often we suppress and hide the memories of people who have hurt us or events in which we were treated unfairly, tucking them away into the closets of the subconscious mind. This holds us back. A chaplain must work on the hidden things in his or her own life so they will be free to help others.

As chaplains, it is important to understand these concepts about unfairness so we are able to effectively communicate in a kind and acceptable way. There are proper times when it is right to explain to people that life was never meant to be fair. However, having this understanding is never a license to be unkind or cruel. When someone has just gone through a tragic event, like losing a child, losing a job, or failing miserably at something, it is not the time to share this knowledge. They need a kind, understanding, and listening ear, and maybe they need to cry on your shoulder.

The human experience is meant to be like the body. When someone is hurting, others help by providing them comfort and initiating the healing process. This is what the body does when one member is hurting; the whole body gives its attention to the hurting member. If bleeding, the blood rushes to the wound to make a life-net of clotting blood to heal the area and stop the bleeding. Chaplains are the life's blood rushing to the wound in times of crisis. Knowing that life is not only unfair and not meant to be fair will help you handle people in hurtful situations.

Chaplains will be exposed to many situations that are not fair and your caring heart can wilt under some situations through grief transference. Grief transference is a transfer that happens when you are coping with people going through great suffering. An example was September 11, 2001, when our country was unfairly attacked. There were so many heart-wrenching stories that the chaplains could not be on duty for more than a few days before they had to be switched with someone else. Hearing these people pour out their grief caused the chaplains to absorb the victims' grief into themselves. It was not a conscious thing but an automatic response for a caring person. The unfairness of it all. The unfairness that the hijackers chose the planes that carried their loved ones. The unfairness that their loved ones were on the stories above where the plane crashed into the buildings. The unfairness of those who made it out and those who did not. This can especially happen in any disaster.

While stressing one part in the thought, "Life is not meant to be fair," let's not overlook an equally important fact that there is profound unfairness in our world which causes deep wounds. Such incidence is when someone is no longer there for you when you needed them the most. Maybe it's a missing parent, a spouse who left, or a friend who walked away.

I remember how some soldiers came back from the Viet Nam war horribly disfigured. There were wives and fiancés who when they saw them in such a horrible condition, could not deal with the trauma. They pulled their rings off of their fingers, laid them on the pillow, and walked out of their lives forever. This kind of disappointing unfairness cuts so deep that the very spirit is wounded.

73

The spirit of a man will sustain his infirmity;
but a wounded spirit who can bear?
Proverbs 18:14

The wounded spirit usually pertains to someone who has been done terribly wrong. It is not so much the life change but the wound purposely inflicted on them by someone else, a wound that screams unfairness, no matter who did it but more so if it came from somebody close to them.

Some unfairness you cannot bear on your own. A spiritual and emotional caregiver is needed to help. I received a wonderful call on Thanksgiving Day, 2017. It was from a man with whom I had walked during a deep dark valley of unfairness in his life. After several years of healing, he has emerged on the other side of his trial into the sunshine of joy and called to thank me for caring during his dark time. This is the kind of thing that warms my chaplain heart.

Some unfairness requires a time of recovery just as deep wounds take time to heal. This is because some unfairness is a deep wound in the spirit. Some people have scars of unfairness they will live with the rest of their lives. World War II left many people with these kinds of scars. The way we process unfairness is important to the very survival of our being.

Our God experienced probably the greatest of all unfairness when He took on the form of a man and walked among the very creatures He created, only to have them reject Him. He was excluded and rejected by His own and persecuted by those professing to serve Him. In exchange for His healing, they beat Him with thirty-nine stripes. For raising their dead back to life, He died at the hands of religious people. Yes, I would say it was greatly unfair. He turned unfairness on its head by willingly dying for those who hated Him. They did not take His life; He gave it freely, allowing Himself to be killed. In doing so, unfairness had no hold.

He came unto his own, and his own received him not. But as many as received him, to them gave he power to become the sons of God, even to them that believe on his name:

John 1:11-12

We all have problems that must be faced, some more unfair than others, but our Creator placed within us the unique ability to arise, meet our problems, and overcome great odds. Like the blade of grass that squeezes through the very smallest crack in the cement, it overcomes something much greater than itself. An overcoming positive attitude will go a long way to help us overcome the "not fair" in life. In overcoming we can stand with others who overcame the odds, like blind and deaf Helen Keller and shout, "This is not fair!" while she graduated cum laude from Radcliffe College.

Life only becomes fair when viewed in the light of eternity. If this were the only life we had, then I would agree with those who say life is not fair, but this is not all there is. In that world to come, things are switched around. All men become equal. The king and the poor man stand together, side by side. We take hope into view of that world which shall be.

In closing this chapter, I would like to point out that by arming yourself with the understanding that life is not fair, nor was it ever meant to be, you will be able to face your own issues with life's unfairness as well as that of others who you are trying to help.

Anger

God and an Angry World

After years of teaching hundreds of people anger management and seeing the great violence in our world, it is no surprise to conclude that we live in an angry world. As a chaplain or someone involved in ministry outside the church, you will need to observe, define and choose carefully how you deal with anger. We cannot fix the world's anger problems, yet we are given unique opportunities to help on the ground level. I have observed when crisis events happen, people tend to become more approachable and may even reach out for help. With sudden unexpected death, a prolonged illness, a disaster strike, or approaching death, a certain vulnerability and honesty will make its way to the surface. I am convinced that many angry people do not want to be angry; they just don't know how not to be angry.

I have a good friend who growing up had enough rejection, abuse, abandonment and total emotional destruction to overwhelm a dozen people. Realizing how much anger had hurt him and others, he made a promise to himself that he would never hurt anyone or drink alcohol. Underneath was a simmering cauldron of anger that was not going to be stopped, even though he had promised himself it would never happen. My friend found himself unable to keep the burning anger contained. Anger has a way of venting, like a lid on a boiling pot, whether you want it to or not. Even contained, it will find a way to the surface sooner or later. This anger can be directed at others or appear in the person's mental, spiritual or physical body. In my friend's case, anger took on the form of hate for other people. Fighting and hurting people became his way of life, and try as hard as he might, he broke every promise he had made to himself. He hurt people physically and struggled with substance abuse. He told me that when he broke his promises to himself, it drove him spiraling down a path toward suicide. I am so glad that a merciful God found him just moments before he ended his life.

Since then, he has been such a blessing and help to many others and has become a great evangelist.

A danger point may arise when sickness or tragedy strikes, especially when it comes suddenly or near the end of a person's life. Angry people tend to see things through an angry viewpoint. This view can lead them to think God is angry at them. If a person believes this about God, it can produce a tendency to draw them away from God rather than toward Him. An example of this is a child in trouble who does not want to see daddy when he comes home. The child wants to hide. What a trap this is! In reality, when in a time of need, we ought to approach God, not draw away from Him.

Let us therefore come boldly unto the throne of grace, that we may obtain mercy, and find grace to help in time of need.
Hebrews 4:16

This chapter can be divided into different streams to indicate who is angry. One stream would be God's anger with man. Another stream would be man's anger with God. The third is anger directed from man to man.

Let's look at the first stream. In some cases, religion has painted God as angry, vindictive and judgmental. Jesus came not to condemn but to save. Human thinking seems to intermingle easily with the idea of an angry vindictive God due to our fallen nature. This thinking can revert back at the most inopportune times, even among Christians who should understand better. Guilt for past wrong doings, or even perceived wrong can cause this. Guilt haunts like a tormenting hunter seeking its prey. God does not have an axe poised to chop off your head.

People living with anger sometimes push their anger down, ignoring it, thinking they have gotten past it, only to have it rush out during crisis. Speaking of inopportune times, chaplains need to be aware that funerals are a prime time for anger to appear, especially from surviving family members. I personally have seen this happen, therefore being prepared for this will help you to quickly bring calm to the situation.

I conducted one funeral where we actually had to guard the body because the widow became so angry at a young lady who showed

> ...we actually had to guard the body because the widow became so angry.

up, she just knew this girl was going to do something to the body. The widow was nearly worried out of her mind; we spent several days working through her chaotic anger. Finally, the young woman left town and went back to her home state, so everything gradually settled down.

Here I would point out that we humans are a sum total of what we were taught, either outright, through experience, by osmosis, or as a result of the decisions we have made or those others have made that have affected us. Every event, memory, joy and disappointment, and even those undone things which are stored on the shelves of life have shaped our emotions and thinking processes. The problem the widow had with this young lady was a failure in the past that connected them through an unresolved conflict. On the shelves of her life were the remains of an anger that had never been addressed. It had laid dormant all those years, then suddenly resurfaced.

In the story of Cain and Able, we find that Cain had anger because God had rejected his sacrifice which he transferred to another person. Cain did not do what was right in God's eyes and because God did not accept what Cain brought as an offering he began to brew over it. His own thinking began to transfer his anger toward God to his brother. Even after God talked with Cain, he still walked down the path of anger, hatred and murder. "Cain, you can change this by doing what is right," was the gist of what God spoke to him. And yet Cain's anger was perhaps beyond the point of turning back. Have you ever been so angry that you wanted to stay angry and not move away from being angry? I have, though not enough

78

to kill someone. But I was angry enough to be glad I was angry and wasn't about to turn around. God told Cain something else; He said, "There is something lurking at the door waiting to pounce on you unless you get a handle on the anger." (Paraphrased) Cain did not get a handle on that anger but allowed it to lead him, becoming the first murderer. This illustrates the danger of letting your anger boil and seethe and remain in your life without dealing with it. We can clearly see how being angry at God can lead to being angry at others, enough so to kill. The scripture fits that says…

Be ye angry and sin not…
Ephesians 4:26

And again…

Whosoever hateth his brother is a murderer …
1 John 3:15

Thinking God is Angry at Them

When dealing with people that believe God is angry with them, remember that chaplains are not there to be the fixer but the bridge-builder. A bridge-builder is a person who sees a need and builds a bridge to that person so that individual can invite you across. Notice that we are to be invited, not rush over. The building of the bridge is a process wherein you help people understand that you care and will listen to them. To help someone unburden their soul of guilt and remorse is one of the greatest gifts an emotional and spiritual caregiver can give.

I remember a true story I heard one of our preachers tell. He spoke of a wonderful couple who had been coming to his church for a few years. They were a great couple, always helpful and supportive of the church. The pastor noticed that they never went to the altar or made a move to grow closer to God in any way. No matter how evangelistic the message was that moved others to seek repentance or baptism, this couple never made any effort. This really bothered the pastor because they were such good and faithful people. The pastor concluded that something must be wrong, so he finally went

79

to them and asked them why they seemingly did not want salvation. Their response shocked the pastor. They said, "You mean we can be saved?" This took the pastor back, not imagining anyone would think they could not be saved. As the pastor inquired further, they told their story. They had been associated with a denomination all their lives which had excommunicated them and told them they could never be saved; God was angry at them, and they were doomed. What joy when they found out they could be forgiven and that God was not angry at them but loved them and wanted to save them.

Angry at God

A person is angry at God. Ministering to people with this kind of anger issue is one of the most difficult undertakings. The question I bring to you, is God big enough for a person to be angry at Him and God still love that person?

Many people have been wounded. This can be a real or perceived hurt, caused by man or even God Himself as was the case with Cain. I believe that kind of anger must have its start with a misunderstanding, perhaps a misconception of how God works or a preconceived notion of how God should have done something. When He does not do something according to the way a person thinks God should do it, then a misunderstanding occurs. This can give way to disappointment, bitterness, frustration, and anger toward others, even anger at God. Perhaps this is not the case for everyone, but looking back, it seems that it was for me. An incident occurred in my young life that led to doubt and confusion, then to anger. At first it was anger toward others; then it was aimed at God. As the years went on it finally turned to total unbelief and then my abandonment of God.

> ...my father died in a plane wreck and was raised back to life.

I have firsthand experience with anger at God so that is probably why I chose to write about this subject. In 1958, when I was nine years old, my father died in a plane wreck and was raised back to life through prayer. In addition to having the right side of his head split open with a brain injury that most people would never have recovered from, his leg had been driven clear through his pelvic bone, paralyzing his hip and leg. After surgery on his head, my father was sent home from the University of Washington Hospital as a hopeless cripple since during the 1950's they did not do hip replacements. He was told that he would never walk again. God healed him without surgery within weeks after leaving the hospital, and he walked for forty some more years. From this, I knew God could do anything.

On the other hand, at the age of twelve and a half, I saw my mother stricken with two kinds of polio and malaria. She was placed in an iron lung, separated from the family, and was totally paralyzed from the neck down. Machines kept my mom alive night and day with every breath pumped in or forced out by mechanical means. My father carried a knife everywhere prepared for the moment he would have to cut a hole in my mother's throat to allow her to breathe if the dreaded emergency occurred. The doctors had told him this very well could happen and that he needed to be prepared. After living with and watching her suffering for close to four years, she died. Here was a missionary that had dedicated her life to the work of God, and yet God allowed this to happen. This is a classic stumbling block, "Why did God let this happen to such a good person?"

When a family member suffers, the family goes through it with them. I suffered with my mom. I was grateful my father had his testimony of God's healing miracle in his life but questioned God as to why He allowed my good mother to suffer and die, taking her away from me.

During both times of sickness with our parents, my older brother and I were shipped off to the grandparents to live. During our father's hospital stay and recovery, the time was shorter than when my mother was taken ill. When she was stricken down we lived

81

away from home for a couple of years. Being pulled away from our parents and shipped off caused an even deeper uncertainty for me.

This became the incident in my life that tilted my faith away from God and also led to horrible confusion. I am sure that many other things factored into this saga, such as turbulent teen years, my own lack of personal experience with God, resentment, and then my own sins. The result was that I became angry at God.

At first, I did not totally fight against God; I just walked away and gave Him no place in my life. However, He did not walk away from me through three tours in Viet Nam, a problem with substance abuse to dull the hurting heart, and a whole lot of sin. Later, my anger became hate, and I remember cursing at God and telling Him to leave me alone on several occasions. Finally, the day came when I no longer believed in God and began to doubt if there was a God. Yet I can say as I look back now, that in all of this, God never left me. I can count at least four times I was in a situation where in all probability I should have died, but God kept me. I got shot down in a helicopter, poisoned, electrocuted by the wild leg of a four-forty buss-bar, and escaped an industrial accident that killed five of my coworkers just one floor below me. To the question, "Is God big enough for a person to be angry at Him and God still love that person?" My answer is, "Yes, He is big enough."

I am not suggesting that chaplains encourage or condone anger at God, but I am saying that God is big enough to handle it and still extend grace. Herein lays a wonderful tool to help the angry soul, expressing the truth of the love of God that will bring hope. I personally believe that angry people need hope to move beyond their anger. If two people are in opposite corners, there is the need for one of them to make the first move, to give in some so the other one can feel safe about leaving their corner. God has done this already by extending grace. He made the first move.

Anger is a God-given emotion restricted to the perimeters that God gave us.

Be ye angry, and sin not:
let not the sun go down upon your wrath:
Ephesians 4:26

Anger can and does become irrational when pushed beyond its rightful boundaries. On one hand, anger can be a God-given catharsis, a liberation to purge or cleanse emotions in a right way. If you are correct in your anger, you can set yourself on a course to right a wrong or stand against an evil. On the other hand, anger can become rage and a spiritual cancer that will consume the soul. However, anger can also become a way of shifting the blame onto someone else and not taking responsibility for your own actions.

My personal experience that God used to turn my heart away from anger and back to Him did not come in a church or with a preacher. After eleven years of wandering, God came to my home during a desperate crisis in my life. What I experienced in my very sinful, angry shape was not that of an angry God, but rather a God who loved me and wanted to help me out of the pit into which I had fallen. It was not the strict laws of God or the teaching of a church that turned my angry heart, melting away the bitterness and much of the hurt. It was not even the threat of going to Hell that made me change my ways. It was the unconditional love of God that I felt for the very first time in my life. That love made me want to never be angry or bitter again. I only wanted to experience that love over and over again. I suddenly had a great desire to please God that was generated by His great love and forgiveness. You see, God didn't wait for me to come to His corner; He came to the corner where I was and showed me He loved me.

A chaplain needs to be the embodiment of the love of God when ministering to the hurting person. When you truly love someone they will know it and they will begin to trust you. Trust should not to be squandered. I can never express enough how important it is to be known as someone who can be trusted to keep confidences. If you break trust, you break more than just a secret. You break their trust in you as someone who will help them, who won't hurt them, and you tear down the bridge you built, losing the invitation that was extended to you.

Rod was the journeyman, and I was the apprentice, so I had to follow him and work beside him many times. He was a mean and obnoxious man and seemed to hate everyone. I can only assume that is why he was on his third or fourth marriage. When you hate everyone, it is hard to have a good relationship with anyone. In time, I discovered that Rod was angry at God which was manifested in hate. It seemed his anger stemmed from the loss of a son. When he died, Rod blamed God for it. One day I told Rod, "I am going to be your friend."

Rod snapped, "I don't want to be your friend."

I said, "Rod, you do not have a choice. I am going to be your friend. Now you have a choice of *if* you are going to be a friend to me, but I am going to be your friend."

Rod did not have a reply to this and I was never able to help him unburden his soul because I changed jobs sometime after that. However, for years afterward, when Rod would see someone who knew me, he would always ask how I was doing. I had built a bridge. Rod would not cross over it, but he would stand on the bridge and call, "Are you still there? I remember you caring, and my heart is crying out for the love I felt."

Anger can hurt and destroy a soul; a root of bitterness will defile it. God can take the anger out of the hurt and comfort the brokenhearted. In my life, the pain of being hurt is still there to some degree, but the anger is gone. Occasionally, I still glimpse a pocket or two that needs to be emptied. It is like a tree that's been cut down to ground level, and after some time, a bunch of little limbs begin growing out of the stump.

One thing I have found is that you cannot be angry at God, yourself, or others without it affecting those around you. This is a tell-tale sign when dealing with people. If someone shows signs of anger toward those around them, then there is a real possibility they are angry at themselves and God. Good people, even Christians who have given up their anger at God long ago, or think they have, can still have wounds that need healing, and as a result may still struggle with some anger, resentment, and guilt.

I am reminded of a man whose story was told to me by an elder minister. The man was the product of a wrong relationship and when he was too young to remember, another man came into his life as his stepfather. This man was angry and hateful to his stepson because he was someone else's child. The mother recounted to her son that as a baby he was lying on the floor crying. His stepfather, who had been drinking, became so angry that he picked up a phone, the old heavy type, and was bringing it down to crush his head when his mother lunged into the stepfather, deflecting the deadly blow. When the blow came, it crushed the baby's hand, missing his head. So the young man grew up with a broken and useless finger.

> ...he picked up a phone and brought it down to crush his head.

After years of rejection and anger, the young man was on his way to Viet Nam and stopped to say goodbye to his stepfather. He said, "Dad, I am going to Viet Nam and I am not sure I will make it back, so I wanted to say goodbye." The stepfather never looked up from his paper or acknowledged that he had spoken. The young man left for the war and the stepfather died shortly thereafter when someone ran over him as he drunkenly walked out in front of their car. The young man never saw his stepdad again. Years later the young man came to know God, became a preacher and served God for many years. One day while in prayer, God asked him a question, "Why don't you ever call me Father?" The preacher said all he could do was hold up his useless finger. Was it anger or hurt? The lines get blurred at times, but whichever it was, it affected his relationship with his heavenly Father. Many people who have a relationship with God still have wounds and hurts that affect their relationship with God.

There is another form of anger that is passive or silent. We may not even know we have it since it lingers under the surface. Our earthly fathers are to be a reflection of our heavenly Father and His love. This is why broken families are so harmful to the young. This anger places a wedge between God and the child. In the case of the young man, it transposed from passive anger at the stepfather to passive anger at God.

Personally, I believe I have traveled this part of the stream also, although quite differently than the young man I just described. I had good parents who provided for me and were not drunken. Sometimes a father is too busy or does not connect with his child. Sometimes he is too harsh of a disciplinarian who may represent an angry God to a child. Whatever the cause, even if it's unknown or unrealized, passive anger can lead to conscious anger at God as it did with me.

The chaplain, in fact anyone in ministry, must first face the anger issues in their own lives before they can effectively minister to others. This takes looking deep inside yourself, into those hidden realms of the mind. Anger can be triggered from outside sources or can be a result of internal self-loathing. Anger at yourself can result from things you have done, sin committed which produces guilt and shame, or just not reaching the level in life to which you thought you should have attained. The secret to helping yourself is a complete honesty with God. Honesty with God? Why not, He knows it anyway, but by facing it and telling it straight up to God, He gives you a freedom you have not previously experienced or known.

Angry Christians

We cannot leave this subject without speaking of vengeance. In its simplest form, vengeance is wanting the bad guy to get his punishment. There's a desire to see the person who has wronged or harmed someone, get what they deserve, pay restitution, or be punished somehow. Yet God says, *"Vengeance is mine; I will repay,"* (Romans 12:19).

Jonah is a good example of this type of vengeance. He wanted the Ninevites dead, wiped from the face of the earth. He was very angry at God for not destroying them. God asked him two times if he did well to be angry. Jonah's exact words were *"I do well to be angry, even unto death."*[11] Being so angry that you would choose to die rather than listen to reason indicates a problematic attitude. We do not know all that was behind Jonah's reasoning except that they were his nation's enemy. There's no doubt that the Ninevites had done much harm to God's people over the years. Historically, Nineveh was known to be a "Sin City." Perhaps Jonah was considering his own reputation, thinking he would be counted as a false prophet because he had prophesied God was going to destroy their city, and it did not happen. We only know what he told God. I will paraphrase what he said; "God, I told you before you sent me that you are slow to anger and that you would repent from destroying them. You are too kind and forgiving, and you always want to have mercy on people. That is why I ran away to Tarshish, and You made me come back and tell them you were fixing to kill them. Now look. You didn't do what you said you were going to do, and I wanted you to kill them." But the Ninevites had repented.

In having a judgmental attitude, we tend to forget that we were once the bad guys, before God had mercy on us. Being angry at God because He did not avenge us in the way we think He should have, is not a good idea. Even though Jonah was angry at God and speaking from a bad attitude, God still reasoned with him. God knows things we do not know or take into consideration concerning our situations. God basically told Jonah, "I have one hundred twenty thousand (120,000) people in Nineveh who do not have my laws or my prophets. They do not know their right hand from their left hand, and should I just kill them when they have repented and turned from the evil that was in their hand?"[12]

---

[11] Jonah 4:9
[12] Jonah 4:11

I had a neighboring pastor, an old prophet who has gone on to meet the Lord, who told us the following story. He said there was a man in his church who had given him a hard time. It seemed at every turn, somehow, this man was causing him problems. The old pastor had gotten to the point that he decided to pray God would just turn this nuisance over to the devil because of all the trouble he had caused. The old prophet said that as he was getting down to pray, but before his knees hit the floor, the Lord spoke to him and said, "What if he were your child?" The pastor said he just got back up and never prayed that prayer. The troublemaker later straightened out and became a missionary to a foreign field, serving the Lord for many years.

Moses himself became so bothered by the people's griping and complaining that he became angry and disobeyed God. The Bible says Moses was the meekest man on the earth, so as a chaplain or a minister, don't think you are above becoming angry. You will need to guard your own mindset and attitude as you are trying to help others.

That reminds me of another story I heard years ago. It seems this pastor had done some fasting and praying about his old man, the flesh. After prayer, he told his wife he felt like he had finally succeeded in "getting this old man under subjection." About that time, he looked out of the window and saw their red hen going down the row of the garden that he had just planted the day before. She was scratching up each of the new plants that he had so carefully planted. He grabbed his wife's broom and chased the red hen all over the garden trying to hit it. When he finally came back into the house, he said to his wife, "I think I have a little bit more work to do on this old man."

Unforgiveness

Unforgiveness is like a cancer of the soul. Left hidden, unforgiveness begins to rot out the insides of a person's being. It can even cause health problems and mental issues. I was dealing with a lady, who from all outward appearances, seemed to be a

88

well-adjusted middle-class housewife. She had come for help with a problem she was having; she had an addiction to prescription medicine. In counseling, I began probing, trying to discover the root of her trouble. We traveled all the way back to her second-grade class. Somehow, her second-grade teacher had embarrassed her and she had never let it go. Immediately, I could see from her reaction that she had deep-set unforgiveness toward this teacher. This was the *root* of her addiction. As we talked, I found out that this teacher was already deceased, so I began to draw attention to the fact that her hatred of the teacher was not hurting the teacher because she was dead. The only person her unforgiveness was hurting was her.

People carry things for years and need help to unload their burdens. Sometimes just listening to them is a great catharsis. Catharsis means purging, cleansing, or removing. Some things can only be released by purging. There is something to be said for telling someone your troubles and having them pray for you, and with you. It is Biblical.

Confess your fault one to another,
and pray one for another, that ye may be healed...
James 5:16

Kinds of purging God has given us include laughter, crying and grieving. But the greatest of all purging is repentance. A great deal can be accomplished in one honest session of repentance to lift years of guilt, regret and shame. This is a particularly wonderful tool when working in a jail or prison. We have led many prisoners to forgive their mothers, fathers, and family members.

Unforgiveness blocks people from obtaining freedom. Normally, I would preach a sermon on repentance and forgiveness and then lead the prisoners in a prayer of forgiveness. I would have them repeat after me, "I forgive the judge who sent me here. I forgive the prosecutor. I forgive the jailer. I forgive my wife who did me wrong. I forgive myself." We can't forget the importance of forgiving ourselves. I have seen people who can forgive everyone else but themselves.

False Guilt

One time I received a call from the sheriff of our county. He asked if I could go see a lady who was just about beside herself with remorse. I will call her name Mary. That day, Mary had received a call from a relative of a neighbor who lived just down the street, asking Mary if she could go and check on her as they were unable to get in touch with their family member. Mary was very busy that morning and really did not have the time, even resenting a bit that she had been asked. The kids had to be taken to school, and other more pressing things needed to be done. Finally, when Mary did get around to checking on her neighbor, several hours had passed. When she walked into the front room of her neighbor's house, Mary found the lady lying on the floor dead. She had been shot though the head. The scene was vicious and gruesome. Something like this can cause a person to go into shock. What had followed for Mary was a great flood of guilt.

> When she walked into the front room... the lady was lying on the floor dead.

Here is the backstory. Her neighbor's daughter was supposed to testify against a man who had committed a very bad crime. He had told her that if she did, he would kill her. The previous night, the man had come to the home of Mary's neighbor to kill the daughter. Finding only the mother, he killed her. The call that came to me from the sheriff sent me to check on Mary and her family.

As I began to listen to Mary, it became clear that I was dealing with trauma, guilt, and vulnerability. Trauma because of how she found her neighbor and how horribleness of the scene. Something this terrible stamps a lasting picture on the mind that will play over and over. Vulnerability because now on Mary's safe block where she lived with her family, their sense of security had been suddenly ripped away. It's not that they weren't as safe as the day before, but when something like this happens close by, the realization comes to life that something like this could also happen in your home. It will

90

take time to work through both the trauma and perceived vulnerability and may even require counseling.

The last effect of the crime was guilt; in Mary's case it was false guilt. The woman had been dead for several hours. Even if Mary had gone right away to her neighbor's house, the outcome would have been the same because the woman was already dead by the time her family called Mary. In talking to her, Mary began to realize that the neighbor did not die because she did not go check on her right away. That left the guilt of not *wanting* to go check on her neighbor. This one was a bit more difficult. Beginning with the way her day started and her normal responsibilities, walking her through all she had to do, it became a question of where she could have inserted the stop to check on her neighbor into her schedule. Being rushed and having an already full plate, it would be natural to feel bothered by being asked to add another thing to her list of things to do. Her reaction was not mean or meant to be hurtful; it was a natural way anyone might have felt under the same circumstances. This seemed to help her quite a bit, but she will still have months of work on the other two results from having been at the crime scene.

An emotional and spiritual caregiver never knows what circumstances they will encounter on any given day, so they must be trained as well as they can be in order to be prepared, and they must have an ability to lean on God. They need to know how to really listen, observe, and pick up on the clues people are giving.

The Art of Listening

When helping people, you must become a great listener. Everyone has a story to tell, and if you listen intently, they will tell it to you. There are ways the subconscious will reveal what is hidden within the soul, if you have the skills to really listen.

The story of the young man and the monk was told to us by our CPE instructor, James Richardson, one morning. I have written it as near to what I remember as possible. Please note, this was an adaptation.

Story of the Young Man and the Monk [13]

There once was a young man who was told that if he went on a certain journey he would gain much wisdom. So he set off walking on his long and tedious trip. The young man traveled for days until he came to a large river running through a deep gorge. There was a clearing where he could see both sides of the gorge and caught sight of the path proceeding upward on the other side of the river. He noticed that the only way across the river was a narrow foot bridge. The worn path ran through the opening, across the bridge, and up the far side of the hill.

As he proceeded, he could see another person coming down the hill on the other side of the river toward him. He looked like a priest or religious person of some sort. As the two of them drew nearer to each other, the young man noticed that it was a monk in a robe. He was carrying something, a rope. As the monk drew closer, the young man could see him beginning to unwind the several coils of rope. Closer they came until they were a few feet apart. The monk held the rope ready with one hand and called out, "Will you hold my rope?"

---

[13] Edwin H. Friedman, *Friedman's Fables,* chapter entitled *The Bridge* (New York, NY, The Guilford Press, A Division of Guilford Publications, Inc. 1990) 10

The young man quite taken aback stuttered, "I guess so."

The monk said "No, you have to promise me you will hold my rope and not let go." To this, the young man agreed and took the end of the rope being held out to him. With that, the monk tied the other end of the rope around his own waist, ran to the edge of the cliff and jumped over the edge. The force on the other end of the rope dragged the young man toward the edge of the cliff.

Finally, the young man managed to get his foot braced on the bridge and with great effort held the now dangling monk. He screamed, "Why did you do that?"

To this the monk replied, "You promised to hold my rope."

The young man straining, screamed back, "I am going to let go!"

The monk shouted back, "You can't! You promised to hold my rope and not let go!"

"I can't hold your rope forever!" shouted the young man.

"Remember if you let go, I am lost!"

(Adaptation from a story entitled "The Bridge" in *Friedman's Fables*.)

At this point my instructor would ask what he always asked as I will ask you. What did you hear?

This chapter is on the Art of Listening, so as you read that story, what did you really hear or read?

There is an art to listening. It is a skill that will serve you well if you really listen and not just surface-listen. Jumping to a conclusion instead of putting all the pieces together as you hear the whole story will greatly hinder your ministry as a spiritual and emotional caregiver.

A person cannot help but tell their story if you are really listening. People have a subconscious tendency, almost compulsion, to tell their story. Of course, Jesus knew this when He said,

> *... for out of the abundance of the heart the mouth speaketh.*
> **Matthew 12:34**

93

The House Model

(First part of this chapter is a listening outline developed by **James Richardson.** Used by permission.)

Listening is an Essential Dimension of Ministry.

Effective listening is a relational way of being with people in ministry.

Listening training offers practical skills

- Needed to effectively engage with people
- Emphasis on basic attending and active listening skills
- As a vital part of ministry

Listening and Caring Skills

No other set of skills is more important for a leader than that of being an effective listener.

- Provides you with powerful reflective, understanding, and interpretive processes
- Enables you to hear what people say
- Both the surface level/deep structural meaning
- Embedded in verbal messages

Example: Someone might say, "I didn't say I was judgingl!"

- They don't want you to think they're judging
- They were judging

Benefits of Effective Listening are as Follows:

- Increase building rapport with another person or group
- Learn how to listen in depth to a person's story and its meaning
- Come to understand the meaning of a person's statement in its context

- Dramatically reduce the errors that occur in verbal and non-verbal communication
- Come to understand your own forms of communication and increase your accuracy in communication
- How to use your mind while someone is talking
- What to do inside yourself

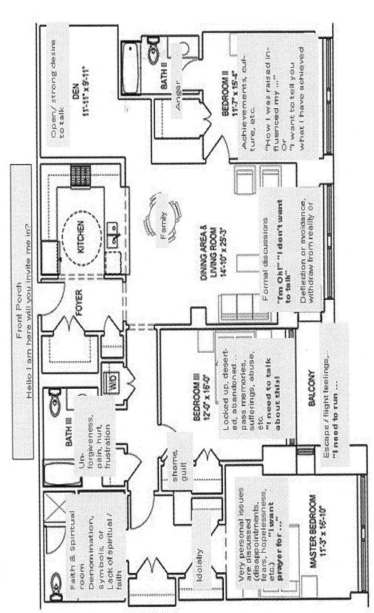

Basement = Family secrets

Attic = family history

Front Porch

Hello I am here will you invite me in?

DEN
11'-11" x 9'-11"

Open / strong desire to talk

BATH III

Anger

BEDROOM II
11'-7" x 15'-4"

Achievements, culture, etc.

"How I was raised influenced my ..."
Or
"I want to tell you what I have achieved

KITCHEN

Family

FOYER

DINING AREA &
LIVING ROOM
14'-10" x 25'-3"

Formal discussions

"I'm-Ok!" "I don't want to talk"

Deflection or avoidance, withdraw from reality or

WD

BEDROOM III
12'-0" x 16'-0"

Locked up, deserted, abandoned... pass memories, sufferings, abuse, etc.
"I need to talk about this!"

BALCONY

Escape / flight feelings...
"I need to run ..."

BATH III

Un-forgiveness, hurt, pain, frustration ...

shame, guilt

Faith & spiritual room
Denomination, symbols, or Lack of spiritual / faith

Idolatry

Very personal issues are discussed (disappointments, fears, hopelessness, etc.)
"I want prayer for ..."

MASTER BEDROOM
11'-3" x 16'-10"

97

We will take each part of this house to explain the following:

- How we listen.
- How we are invited into each room.
- What they are saying when they invite you into another room.
- What they are saying if they do not invite you.
- Finally, what level you are at in each room.

The Porch

Standing on their front porch, you are knocking on the door of their life. You are saying that you care and are ready to listen. You begin establishing your compassion for them at first contact. You may only have said, "How are you?"

For chaplains and ministers, this is more than a question. By the way you look someone in the eyes and speak to them, you are saying, "I am ready to journey with you into the rooms of your life."

Depending on what they are experiencing at the moment, either a troubled or joyful heart, they may invite you into their home. This may be relative to the feelings and thoughts they are experiencing.

The conversation going forward is based on respect for us as established so far in our meeting. This determines how much of the house you will see.

The Living Room and Dining Area

In this room they want to be formal or official with you. This is where family business is discussed and decisions are made. They may want to discuss a family situation, problems or needs.

The Game Room

If they invite you into the game room, they may want to relive their big game. Perhaps they were a college sportsman and they enjoy talking about achievements. Their career or some other important event in their life is talked about here. When they invite you into this room, it signals they are feeling good and are willing to reveal details. This can also be safe small-talk, not yet ready to discuss their real problems.

The Family Room

If they invite you to the Family Room, they are signaling that they want to talk about needs and relationships with their immediate or extended family members. At this point, you need to help them speak openly with open-ended questions like, "How is Johnny doing?" Or, "How are things at work?"

The Job Room

When taken into this room, they want to share with you what they are receiving in life, what they are meaning, or what is their purpose, such as a job or spouse. On the other hand, they may not be receiving any satisfaction or fulfillment, and want to share that as well.

The Marriage Room

Here, the ups and downs they are experiencing in their relationships will be discussed.

The Religion and Faith Room

They will take you to this room when they want to discuss their relationship with God, or whatever they value most at this moment in time.

Hidden Locked Rooms

Most people rarely visit their private rooms. Some do not go because of the pain or the emotions going there evokes. Getting them to invite you into this area takes a bit of probing.

You may have asked an open-ended question like, "What is your greatest fear?"

As they reflect on your question, they will journey back into that dark room. The expression on their face sometimes give them away, and occasionally there will be tears mixed with deep emotions. It might be unresolved grief they have not allowed themselves time to process. It could even be un-confessed sin, etc.

The Closets of Life

In these closed off places, things placed here may seem like insignificant things to that person. They have managed to tuck them away long ago so as long as they are unable to see them or be reminded, they feel that life is good. There could be a past misunderstanding or broken relationship stuck back in the corner. Yet these forgotten or put away things are still alive and well in the subconscious and can hinder them.

The Balcony

If you feel they are leading you to the balcony they are saying, "I am feeling uncomfortable and want to escape." At this point, you need to allow them some kind of leeway by changing the subject and trying again some other time. Once you have lost your invitation, they will close down on you, even if they are still being polite.

The Attic

Here you will find out the history of each person in the family. This affects how a person reacts and thinks about circumstances presently being experienced. This can point to why they are thinking or reacting to circumstances the way they are. This guides you in how to approach certain subjects or issues.

Following is an example of a man who had tucked away a family tragedy from years before, not knowing he only knew part of the story.

John was raised in a Christian home. The family attended church in the neighborhood regularly. One day his big brother fell off the back porch and broke his neck. After the funeral, the family stopped attending church. John never could understand why the family ceased going to church. Now that he is a grownup and has his own family, none of his kinfolk will discuss this terrible day with him, and he wanted to know, "Why?"

The Basements of Life

The basements of life represent family secrets. This may or may not have been understood, but secrets are most often not talked about by the family.

What John discovered later in life was that his mother had pushed his big brother off the porch in anger. She did not know her act would break his neck. His big sister and father knew this hidden secret. The mother fell into a deep depression, never seeking help. She had forced the

> She did not know her act would break his neck.

father and sister into secrecy. This caused the family enormous pain until the mother committed suicide. Then the father told the story he had suffered most of his life in silence. The older sister ended up on the streets, drinking her way through life. A chaplain never knows somebody's sorrows until they listen.

No One is Pushing

They have to lead you; do not lead them. Don't push them in the direction you think they should go. This is harder than you think, especially when you believe your answer might help them. They must lead the way. Only then will you be invited into other rooms. Only then will you be trusted with their deepest needs.

If you are invited into someone's house it would never be right or proper to say, I think I will go into your den, I want to see what is in there. No, you wait to be invited, and so it is with listening.

Taking a Closer Look

Listening and Caring Skills will provide you with:

(1) Powerful reflective, understanding, and interpretive processes that will enable you to hear what people say at

(2) Both the surface level and the deeper, internal level that is embedded in their verbal messages.

101

Let's look at powerful, reflective understanding and interpretive processes. Considering only the words that are spoken gives you an incomplete understanding of what is being said. Only a part of what needs to be conveyed is spoken. If you add tone and expression, this still gives you only a portion of the message. (Note: Communicating without being in person can lead to all kinds of misunderstandings because you do not have the advantage of tone and expression, let alone other listening skills.) When a story is being told, if you are really hearing using the skills of an active listener, you will be able to gain greater understanding as well as broaden your effectiveness.

Secondly, hearing on both the surface and a deeper internal level will bring structural meaning that is embedded in the verbal messages. This brings a deeper understanding of what is really going on inside the person. Someone saying *yes* and shaking their head *no* at the same time indicates that there is more to the *yes* than what is being expressed.

Bad Habits in Listening

When I was child we were taught that children were to be seen and not heard. You would have thought that should have made me become a great listener. But it did not. Perhaps it became a compressed sponge effect. Finally given a chance to talk, I was getting even for all my years of silence, just kidding.

School Took its Toll

School demands you to mostly listen so this should have been another chance for me to learn to be a great listener.

School's emphasis was placed on gaining information, as much and as fast as it was spoken or read. This was boring to a lot of kids, and especially me. Looking back, I can see that I was ADHD (Attention Deficit Hyperactive Disorder) long before it was understood as a disorder. "Listening only" was very boring to me, so I did not gain listening skills in school.

Adding to this, research studies have shown that only about seven percent of what is spoken is retained. All studies I have seen show a pretty low percentage of verbal-only retention.

Short-cuts

By hearing the spoken words only, we develop bad short-cut habits. The problem comes from picking out things the mind tells us are important points while cutting out what we deem less important. This is done on the subconscious level unless trained to avoid this habit. It is kind of like speed reading where you do not read every word. Instead, you let your mind fill in the blanks. In listening, the same problem can occur. Your mind can just block out things when it assumes the meaning instead of really listening.

Mind-Drift

When people are talking, there is a danger of letting your mind drift. Perhaps it was the teacher who yelled at me in my third or fourth grade class. Out of my assigned desk once again. She must have told me several times to stay in my seat, but I don't remember. In a very loud and sharp voice she said, "Billy, if you get out of your desk one more time, I will tie you in your seat with the jump rope." That got my attention and so traumatized me that I swore I would never again get out of my seat. Five minutes later, I was on my way to the pencil sharpener when she yelled at me again. My mind had drifted, again. I had totally forgotten her threat and my swearing to never leave my seat again. Busted, betrayed by my own drifting mind, and it wasn't that I did not hear her because I really did. Still, somehow my mind had skipped a cog or something.

Probably in your case your mind does not drift as greatly as mine does, but to some extent you are losing great opportunities to understand people by having mind-drift. Relearning how to truly listen is the first step in combatting this.

Distractions

We get interrupted. We can't get focused because we are thinking about something else. It is not that we do not hear, but more accurately, our mind is racing over many other things. Consequently, we forget many things in a conversation. Maybe we are not entirely hearing the conversation because of distractions. Possibly we are not totally listening because we are thinking of what we will say just as soon as we can get a word in edgewise.

Another distraction that causes our minds to wander might be something someone says which sparks a memory we want to share with them. We want to tell our story, so much so that we block out what the other person is saying so we won't forget what we have to say.

Distraction of the Above Average Talker

Everyone knows a person you could label as the above-average talker. Generally, the talker is a very outgoing person, someone who has a fun personality and is likely to be the life of the party. That person has to be doubly careful to talk less and listen more. I have a very neat granddaughter, who got in trouble in class. She kept cracking jokes causing the whole class to laugh, upsetting her teacher. Her mother asked her, "Why didn't you quit when the teacher corrected you?"

She replayed, "I just had so many neat things to say, they just kept popping out."

Fear of What We Will Say

Another bad listening habit is based in fear. We don't want to look dumb, be put on the spot, or be left without a defense.

> We don't want to look dumb, be put on the spot...

In school I dreaded being put on the spot. Consequently, that dread caused me to acquire another bad habit. As I was listening, I was also trying to think of what to say. So I am nailed again. My dread happens. I am called upon in class, and I have to give an answer. As I stammer out the answer, I find that it was the correct answer, but to the third question previously asked. Then the

104

teacher would say, "You weren't paying attention, Billy." I really was, but there wasn't room in my head for both conversations at the same time, so I missed the part I needed. Unfortunately, it was the part that held the right answer.

Are you Listening Young Man?

"Are you listening to me young man?" The stern look on my father's face told me I was about to get into big trouble. My mind was already racing to my defense. Quick! Come up with something! Get out of this fix! I was not fully listening, because I was desperately searching for something, anything to help me out. This habit has caused me to have even bigger big problems. Not only was I not fully listening, but my defense was not so good because I only had half the understanding of what had been said. My answer might have been correct a few minutes ago except for the distractions of not fully listening.

That is not Comfortable

The major emphases of Clinical Pastoral Education (CPE) is to dig out anything that could cause you to shy away from areas that make you uncomfortable.

Say you had a traumatic childhood experience in which you were exposed to the death of a close family member as I had been. I never realized what I had buried deep inside my subconscious. When listening to someone, there is a tendency to avoid or change the subject when approaching an uncomfortable subject. When someone was telling their story, and the subject approached the same undealt with hurt I had buried, my subconscious defense mechanisms kicked in. Usually, I would interrupt their story and take over the driver's seat, steering the conversation away from the hidden matter tucked away in the deep chasms of my brain. This was all done on a subconscious and automatic level. In CPE we learn how to listen, probe, counsel, and search our inner self, yet no one has ever discovered everything they have suppressed; it is always a work in progress.

105

We can work at recognizing our wounds that keep us from really listening to others. I recommend the book *The Wounded Healer* by Henri J. M. Nouwen, which deals with the subject of ministering to others with wounds of your own.

Paradigm Thinking

Paradigm thinking is defined as the particular pattern in the way you think. It is the customary way you see, hear, and perceive things. It is a standard in your mind.

We all have them. Yours may be different than mine but we all have them. Our minds draw on things from the past that seem normal to us. It's like little boxes, or what I call pigeon holes, where we put stuff in our minds. These pigeon-holed things are matched and compared quicker than we can even consciously think. By matching, our mind tries to find the right pigeon hole for the newly introduced information. This causes a problem when something is said that does not match anything you have experienced or anything for which you have any previous knowledge.

Years ago I watched a training video on paradigms. It proved that the mind shifts some realities to fit a certain way of perception. It was shocking to me as I watched my own mind shift things that were plainly not as I thought I had seen them once my attention was drawn to focus on them.

A Paradigm Deck of Cards

A deck of cards became distorted by my mind. It didn't fit the paradigm of what my mind said was correct. They had changed the colors. The spades were red and the hearts were black. The cards were shown to me one at a time, at a readable rate. Then, they slowed down the visual exhibition going through the deck the second time. My mind still saw a typical deck. Why? Because my paradigm was *forcing* my mind to see what it believed *should* be a normal deck of cards but not what it was *really* seeing. To change our way of thinking about something, we have to change our paradigm.

The Same Can Be True When Listening

Our minds can subconsciously change things unless we train our minds to hear the whole message. I have read many author's thoughts on listening who say to let your mind eliminate the less important parts and concentrate on the most important elements. I cannot see that this helps anything except to make it easier to retain the key points. By doing this you may also slip into your own paradigm thinking and misinterpret what has really been said.

Written in Tony Campolo's book, *Let me Tell You a Story*, Tony Campolo tells of teaching a class in which he shouted out to an unsuspecting student, "How long have you lived?"

The young man said, "I am twenty-two years old."

Dr. Campolo responded, "You just told me how long your heart has been beating. I asked you, how long have you lived?"

The young man had missed the point. He had fallen into the trap of responding according to what his mind said should have been the answer. The normal pattern for a question that fit his response should have been, "How old are you?" The mind exchanged the words, "How long have you lived?" for "How old are you?"

Now that we have touched on things that keep us from really listening to others, let us look at some of the skills that can help us go even deeper into what is actually being said.

Building Bridges and Trust Levels

In many cases, building bridges takes time, but when there is no time for construction, there are still tools that can help you. For example, you are going to the hospital to visit a stranger. You do not have a lot of time to build that bridge. By observing the room, you can find some building materials. This can get you past the front porch.

You have just walked into their room. The lights are dim, the shades are closed, and the door is shut. There is a worried look on the patient's face. Perhaps they are depressed or have just received a bad report. Looking further there is no evidence that anyone has been to visit. There are no clothes, baskets of goodies, or anything else that indicates visitors. This tells you that they are not from your area, do not have family in the vicinity, that there might be a rift in the family, or that they might be without a family.

With this clue you might ask, "Has anyone come to see you?" or

"Where have you lived most of your life?"

On one hospital visit, after observing that it appeared the patient had not been visited, I asked the question, "Has anyone been up to visit you?" This caused the man to blurt out, "I haven't talked to my kid in a year." Now I knew where some of the problem was and what to ask next. This does not happen as often as we would like, but his answer that day was saying, "I have flung open the door and y'all come on in; we will talk." By the end of our several visits, he had spoken with his son.

> "I haven't talked to my kid in a year."

Developing a Skill Set

Reading Between the Lines

It is not so much what is said but how it is said. What was left out? What does the body language say? What other observable clues are there? Reading between the lines takes many different skills to hear the whole story.

Skill Number One: Missing Information

Broken or partial information leaves out vital details.

Example:

I am really upset with the meeting yesterday; seems like they never know how to run things.

Here is what you were not told.

1. What meeting?
2. Who was there?
3. Who does not know how to run things?
4. What things?
5. What made you upset
6. How could the meeting have gone better?

Although it is not the scope of this lesson, this skill is also used in conflict resolution.

Skill Number Two: Open Ended Questions

To find out more information, ask open-ended questions.

Closed-ended questions are those which can be answered by a simple "yes" or "no." Open-ended questions require greater thought and more than a simple one-word answer.

Example

I understand that you were upset yesterday; can you tell me about the meeting?

Skill Number Three: Use of Silence

Having trouble getting a person to open up and talk to you? Try silence. One skill I learned in sales is that you ask a question and then just stand there smiling, looking at them. Try it sometime. It is much harder and more uncomfortable than you might think. The urge is for you to fill the empty space with something. Do not do it. This is a tool compelling them to tell more of their story. It causes a bit of discomfort and awkwardness. While you are not there to make them uncomfortable, it is really just a bit of coaxing through the silence that helps get the ball rolling. Most people will feel compelled to begin telling you their story.

Skill Number Four: Echoing Other Skill Numbers

Summarize what they said and use open-ended questions to clarify what you think you heard. You do not have to use the same exact wording. Shorten it, putting what they said in your own words.

Example

Listener: I think you said that the three of you, John, Sue and yourself were meeting about the Mason project yesterday; is that right?

Speaker: Observably somewhat reluctant to talk about it, says nothing.

Listener: Using silence, looking directly at them with an anticipating look waiting for the answer.

Speaker: Well, yes it was John, Sue and myself at the meeting, and you know how phones are.

Listener: Correct me if I am wrong, but John was running the meeting and kept taking phone calls?

Speaker: Yes, it was John running the meeting, but it was Sue who kept taking phone calls.

Notice How You Were Given Corrected Information

Listener: So you think that if John had told Sue to turn off her phone things would have worked better?

Speaker: John did say something to Sue but only once; he let it go, and that is no way to run a meeting. It was a mess.

Listener: Would it be safe to say that you feel like your time was wasted and this upset you?

Speaker: Yes, it really bothered me and I have been upset ever since.

Now you have a much clearer picture. You used the combination of open-ended questions, silence, and echoing. This checks out if you had correctly pulled together the verbal story.

Skill Number Five: Body Language Tool

Body language tools can tell you many things. What a person is feeling, if they are comfortable, uncomfortable, closed, or open. Reading body language can tell if they are nervous, upset, mad, sad, lying, or telling the truth.

Notice eye contact, and actions of looking while talking and listening, frequency of glances, patterns of fixation, pupil dilation and blink rate, to give you clues. This tool is not meant to challenge them but rather help you understand what is really being said and meant.

Example

Why are they smiling at a sad story? Smiling while telling you they just buried their brother-in-law does not fit normally. Body language is just one of many tools than can alert you to what's going on behind the words. This tool is helpful to get to the truth by exploration. Use these tools without letting the person know what you are doing, otherwise most people will shut down on you. A direct accusation of lying causes shut-down because they stop trusting you. There has to be a certain level of trust for people to talk openly since doing so makes them feel vulnerable and exposed.

Body language helps you discover clues from a person's behavior which can help identify issues more accurately, more than trying to determine a speaker's internal thinking and feelings by guessing and probing with questions.

Downside to Reading Body Language

The better you are at reading body language the more you tend to rely on it. This can cause a greater chance of error; therefore, body language should only be one part of the many tools you use in listening. Here is the reason why. Remember the man who just buried his brother-in-law? You might take his gesture of smiling to mean he did not like his brother-in-law, or maybe he even had something to do with his demise. About the time you jump to this conclusion he adds, "Oh I just remembered something neat and kind of silly that he and I did when we were younger. Those were a lot of good times."

Body language alone is not enough to paint the picture; it is only a few strokes in that unfinished painting.

Some Things not as Easy to Identify

An angry person is not hard to spot no matter what they are saying. You notice that something is wrong and you ask "What is wrong?" The answer comes back, "nothing." You notice the answer is spit out and cut short. The eyes are blazing and the jaw is set. It does not really matter what the person said; their behavior says they are angry. However, you do not know why they are angry, or to whom it is directed, or what caused the anger.

It is an unfinished picture. I won't take the time to go further into Body Language. There are several good books on the subject and you will need a lot of practice to become proficient. You might even want to take some kind of class to more fully understand.

Skill Number Six: Storytelling and Edging Closer

The use of metaphors and figures of speech tells meanings beyond the words that are spoken. The subconscious mind works many times faster than the conscious mind. It keeps pulling things out of our past and hiding things to protect us emotionally. Still, in all of this, the subconscious mind cannot help itself from telling its story.

The Speaker starts to speak and the listener begins by hearing the words. Body language skills help to detect any emotions and meanings that are not being said.

"I can remember when I was a child," the speaker begins as a big smile begins to spread across their face. This tells you there's a fond memory attached to what they are telling you.

"When I was in high school." Now a lonely look or tensing up might indicate negative emotions connected to what they are telling you. If they blush there may be some embarrassment attached.

Shifting of the voice from front of the mouth then to the back of the mouth or even to the throat indicates deep emotions.

The subconscious is telling the untold story. It cannot help telling as it is a subconscious reaction.

Paul Gave us an Example

If Paul was just being humble, it still gives us a great example of storytelling. "I knew a man" story is an allegory form of storytelling.

I knew a man in Christ above fourteen years ago, (whether in the body, I cannot tell; or whether out of the body, I cannot tell: God knoweth;) such an one caught up to the third heaven.
2 Corinthians 12:2

This one is pretty clear that he is talking about himself. What about the person who says…?

"I have a friend who has struggled for years with jealousy and it is ruining his life. How do you think he can overcome this?"

Is this really a story of another person or is there something more to it? Possibly the individual asking about his friend is referring to himself.

113

Rapid Body Signals

As the person tells their story, there might be rapid body signals. This alone is not enough, but it can clue you to ask questions. Perhaps you ask, "Do you have a very close relationship to this person?" If there are no rapid body signals, and the person says, "No," it most likely is not himself. If the opposite is true, then you are probably reading it right.

Rapid body signals like shifting uncomfortably or a shocked look at your question, all give you pieces to your picture. Stammering or tripping over words, quick looking away, or hesitating on the answer, indicate the subconscious is giving valuable clues for the practiced listener.

According to John Savage in his book, *Listening and Caring Skills*, "adults tell [stories] when sharing with another person part of their own life journey."

He sums up this storytelling to five types.

The Five Types of Stories [14]

1. Reinvestment Stories; Tells of shifting commitments and loyalties.
2. Rehearsal Stories; Tell of events in your past life which you retell to inform the listener of what is going on now in your life.
3. "I know someone who" stories; Project your inner conditions onto someone else or some object.
4. Anniversary Stories; Are a type of rehearsal story told at a given time of year, to deal with the unfinished pain or joy of that event.
5. Transition stories; Contains the themes of endings, confusion, and beginnings.

---

[14] John S. Savage, *Listening and Caring Skills, A Guide for Groups and Leaders*, (Nashville, TN, Abingdon Press, 1996) 82

Skill Number Seven: Giving Worth to Others

One of the greatest things you can do for someone is give them your full attention. Listening starts with giving them your full attention. This tells them they are worth listening to, what they have to say is important, and you care enough to hear them.

Not Giving Full Attention

I can remember being at a large meeting where one of our top officials had just closed out the session. I needed just a few moments of his time so I approached him right after the meeting. As I was talking with him, I noticed he kept looking over my shoulder at someone. His body language was telling me that he really wanted to talk to someone else. Perhaps that other person had more of a need than I did. Maybe a death in the family or something I did not know about. And it would have been fine if he had said something like, "I really need to talk with so and so; they have had a death in the family, and I will call you later." That was never conveyed. When he was not interested enough to give me eye contact, I knew what I was telling him was not going to be heard. When I perceived that, I just stopped talking. Then I did the polite thing which was to let him go. I never tried to converse with him again about my concerns and problems for which I needed assistance. People recognize quickly whether or not you are interested, and if you care enough to hear their story.

One thing I believe everyone is craving is a good sense of their own worth or value. If the chaplain truly cares about the people to whom they are ministering, they will be successful. The people to whom you are ministering will probably be the first to recognize you care. They will reward you with trust and will be more open with you.

Just a few days ago while writing this chapter, we received the news that Billy Graham had died. As I listened to the many people who spoke many glowing words about him, I

> Billy Graham was visiting men who had been wounded in war.

115

was struck by one person's recollection in particular. It was on the radio so I could not rightly say who it was that said it. They said Billy Graham was visiting men who had been wounded in war. He came to a man who was on the type of bed where they turn you upside-down facing the floor. Billy Graham got down on the floor and crawled under the bed so he could face the man. The famous evangelist said, "I just came to tell you that Jesus loves you." With that, the man's tears began to fall on Billy Graham. That was real caring that told this man, you are important, worth taking the time to hear, and I am ready to listen.

In Summation...

The house model for listening key points

- Being invited into the rooms of their lives
- The different rooms explained
- How to know what they want to tell you
- Following not leading

How do we become better listeners?

- Mind-drifts
- Distractions
- Thinking what we want to say
- Uncomfortable subjects for us
- Paradigm thinking

Then we talked about tools

- Building bridges and trust levels
- Reading between the lines
- Missing information
- Open-ended questions
- Use of silence
- Echoing
- Body language
- Story telling
- Giving worth to others

This in no way scratches the surface of this great listening tool. In-depth study and practice is needed.

The Young Man and the Monk Story Finished

At the first of this chapter, I asked you, "What did you hear when you heard the story of the young man and the monk?"

I never told you the answer on purpose as I wanted you to think deeply of what you had heard. Jesus used this same method when He said the Kingdom of heaven is like a man sowing seed. Later His disciples asked Him what the parable meant. [15]

The deeper meaning from the monk story explained. The rope is what people try to get you to hold. Some people will try to get you to hold all of their problems and crises situations. They want you to hold their rope so that their load is on you and off of them. They want you to feel obligated and responsible for their problems in life. Once you agree to hold their rope, if you let go, it will be your fault and not theirs if they crash and burn in life. Moral of the story. Help people, but do not agree to hold their rope. People's choices and problems belong to them and taking all their problems upon yourself does not help them; it enables them. This is the great wisdom that the young man gained on his journey.

What Do You Do with This Rope?

I once had a person tell me they had a dream about me. In the dream they saw me talking about them behind their back. They were now convinced that I had been talking about them. How do you help that person and how do you get yourself off the hook for something that they imagined? Knowing this person, I am sure they believed that God had given them this dream to expose my evil deed. Back then I did not have the understanding that could have helped me know better how to handle this.

Open discussion can bring things into a better understanding. I asked her to tell me what I was saying behind her back. She replied,

---

[15] Matthew 13:1-23, Mark 4:1-20, Luke 8:4-15

"I don't know. I did not hear what you were saying, but I know you were talking about me."

I should have noticed the person backing up, just a small movement backward. This indicated fear that I was going to hurt them. Probing questions from a relaxed stance might have worked. I did ask, "What makes you think that I was talking about you if you did not hear what I was saying?"

She replied, "Well it was who you were talking to that made me believe that you were talking about me."

I continued, "So the person who I was talking to in your dream is a person you know talks about you behind your back? And because I was talking to them, you believe that I am talking about you behind your back as well?"

Finally, we got to the heart of the matter. She answers, "Yes, that is right."

Here I am on trial for something I did not do but this lady is convinced I did. There was not much I could say at that point as I did not have some of the skills I have now. I should have helped her think through her dream. It could have gone like this.

You know, you are probably right. I do talk with them. As pastor I talk to everyone in the church, so why if I talked to that person, would you assume that I was talking about you?

Sometimes you have to help a person think through their own story. Here, the rope was not mine to hold. I did not dream the dream. I had not been talking behind her back. Had I taken the rope and held it, she would have jumped off the cliff with it, and it would have been my problem. No, the problem belonged to her.

Everyone Has a Story to Tell

We have discussed many topics, given examples, and talked about tools to use in your ministry. Finally, people's stories are important, not that you want to know their secrets, but rather it is a tool to help understand the way they see the world, giving you a glimpse into how they think and their emotional make-up. It helps you get beyond the façade, or the smokescreen, into the real person so you can build a bridge that you may be invited across.

I told of losing my mother to the work of God when I was a teenager and her four years of suffering. By knowing this you can understand more about how I see things and how I might react in certain situations. Where I am more vulnerable and might need a more cautious approach. Perhaps even seeing areas where there are still open wounds that might need help in healing. Some people are terrified of water, therefore you could easily assume something has caused this. I once baptized a young girl who desperately wanted to be baptized but was afraid of water. I had to catch her off-guard and suddenly immerse her, and she still fought like a wounded wild cat. She was not just putting on an act; she was terrified. This tells you that she still had not healed from some kind of wound. Below, I have laid out some of my story so you can see how gleaning from an assessment about someone's life or story can be helpful.

There are gaps in my story of about eleven years that I have left out. They were painful years brought on by confusion and my own mistakes. This will give you insight into some of my life. I wrote these details on the other side of those eleven years when I had passed through the dark valley and emerged with leftover scars, after God had been so merciful to me.

It was World War II in the South Pacific Islands; the scream of bombs falling pierced the air. The desperate cry of a young man entered into the ears of the Lord, "Save me and I'll serve you!" With one frantic, desperate dive, the young man landed in a foxhole just as the roar of death showered the ground where he had been standing.

It was now the 1950's, and the young man was in his 30's and had planted the first United Pentecostal Church in the Seattle, Washington, area. A burden, stirred by a Godly wife's prayer, began burning in the heart of my father. His cry was, "God, anywhere but there!" meaning the Pacific Islands.

Her cry was, "God, I'll part my hair down the middle as a vow until you send me to the mission field." And so she did.

He prayed until the call came from the Foreign Mission's Department; my parents were appointed to go to the Philippine Islands.

Flying back from a conference in a small plane, unexpectedly they flew into a fog bank in the Black Hills of Washington state. Thick drops of water hung in the air like a blanket ready to smother the little plane piloted by one of our church members. Alongside him was the newly appointed missionary to the Philippines, my father.

Panic seized the new pilot as the plane dove toward the earth. Not knowing which way was up or down, the plane was on its own, the altimeter turning wildly. Whether it was God or man, I cannot tell, but with his own hands and a prayer, the missionary grabbed the controls of the plummeting plane and pulled back just in time to miss a fence post by a mere eight feet. No one knew that the struggle for thousands of souls was being played out in a lonely, fog-drenched valley.

A crash landing was attempted three times, and on the third attempt, the wing hit a tree and the little plane pancaked. The missionary died before ever reaching the mission field, but God was not ready to quit. As the missionary was ascending toward heaven, he looked over his left shoulder and saw

As the missionary was ascending…he saw his body as it lay on the broken wing.

his body trying to get up, but it just lay on the broken wing. The head was broken open and the left leg was driven completely

120

through the pelvic bone. It was no use; the earthly vessel had given up the ghost.

The slightly injured pilot jumped out the other side of the plane and ran to the lifeless shell of the missionary who was now very far from this earth and in a wonderful presence that felt so good. Looking down one last time at the pitiful sight, the power of prayer in Jesus's name by a praying pilot was witnessed as that body was brought back to life.

You see, God was not finished yet!

The missionary's skull was completely split open and had to have a steal plate installed and his skull wired together with stainless steel wire. Months of pain, hospital care, children being sent to relatives, wife dispatched to find a job and hold the church together, she cried, "I was willing to go; why do I struggle so?"

So the Contest Went On; The Stakes Were High

"I am sorry, Mrs. Dillon; your husband will never walk again."

Hey, doctor from the University of Washington Hospital! Didn't anyone tell you that our God never gives up? God spoke to the missionary, "I am going to heal you." Not only did he walk again without surgery, but he preached the gospel where no other missionary had ever gone. Confident of the promise God had given, the missionary crawled out of his hospital bed by faith. He crawled everywhere he went for more than two weeks; after that he was healed. When that round was over, the enemy had to release his hold on the man of God. He continued to walk for thirty-nine more years!

If I Cannot Prevail Against Him, Surely I Will Destroy His Wife

From the darkness of the sidelines came the beginning of a fierce struggle for the very life of the missionary's wife. They had only been in their beloved land of calling two and a half years.

Before she went in prayer, God had gently told my mother, "You will only be there a half-term; do you still want to go?"

"Yes, Lord, I will go."

121

Did she know that her own life would be snuffed out like the slow drowning of an animal in a flooding cellar? Was there knowledge that she would never again hold her baby girl still in diapers, kiss her little boy of five, or hug her fourteen-year-old son and twelve-year-old son, me? Did she realize she would linger four suffering years being paralyzed and helpless without the ability to even breathe except by machines? No, she did not know, nor did she know why she would only be permitted to remain on the mission field for such a short time.

On what altar did she place her widower-to-be husband and children who would become confused and bitter, some not yet having received the Holy Ghost? It was God's altar, you know, the one that is not so pretty. It is rough and shaped like a cross. It is the altar of "love for souls." And the battle raged on.

The Next Rounds Seemed to Go to the Enemy

It began with a pain in her back. The work in Mindanao was newly established. A church had been born in our home and other homes in outlying areas from the reading of a simple tract.

> "It's polio of the worst kind. No, it's two kinds, and malaria too.

"It's polio of the worst kind. No, it's two kinds, and malaria too," came the word back from the doctors. This was to be the one-two-three punch that would bring the missionaries down. The tentacles of death slithered toward the

fragile soldier embracing her body. Emergency, SOS... the call went out. The U.S. Air Force flew in a rescue plane with an iron lung, but she was too sick to travel with them. So they left as the heavens rumbled with a terrible typhoon.

The power was out for days. Back on. Then off again. The figure of a lone missionary stood fighting off death for eighteen days.

Every time there was another electrical power outage, my father had to manually pump every breath into his wife's body for days with little or no sleep. Now she is gone, but not before saying, "Daddy, sing 'America the Beautiful' to me." Then she closed her eyes. The doctors came running to join the fight. They brought her back. She would see America again. "It is not enough!" Satan seemed to say.

Had the Enemy Won? Had God Thrown in the Towel?

The missionaries could no longer stay in the land they loved. Years of hospital and doctors, children separated and shuffled off to live with relatives, feelings of rejection and confusion. All of this soon bore its fruit. Satan did not care. He does not fight fair. It makes no difference to him. He will crush a flower or a bud. The age of a person matters not.

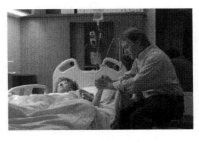

After two years my mother was taken out of the iron lung and placed on other machines that pumped air into her lungs, giving her life. Given back the use of only three fingers on her left hand, not even the arm itself, the missionary's wife wrote a small book while machines enabled her to breathe. It was deemed of little importance. Why publish it? Who would buy such a work? As she wrote the last page and typed the last period she said, "Daddy, my work is done." That very week the earth cried and the heavens rejoiced as she was laid to rest beneath the sod.

Hew Down the Tree and Cut Off the Tender Shoots

Bitterness is seemingly sweet wine to a dying soul, not knowing that it is to their own destruction that they sup. Squeezed from the bitter grapes of misunderstanding and confusion, its nectar flowed into the cup of our lives. "Why, Lord, why?" Now the bitterness progressed, encasing the children. Satan seemed to say, "Why stop at the missionaries when I can have their children too?" Like the kings of old, Satan set out to destroy all the royal seed. But this time Satan had overplayed his hand. Did he not know? The missionary's wife had left her most precious possessions on God's altar. Now, God was taking care of what she could not.

God Never Forgets One of His Children's Prayers

Slowly with reaching hands, God pulled one, then another of those children out of the mire. For forty plus years now I have been preaching the gospel, reaching to a lost world. Two of the missionaries' children are now preaching the same gospel, one married a preacher, and the other one is still where she left him, on God's altar.

Long ago the bitterness and hatred toward God healed, yet I was still not permitted to understand "Why, Lord, why?"

Thirty-three years had passed since my father had laid his wife in the ground. Now the old missionary also dies.

The Dream

It came one night in a dream as God pulled back the curtain of time to reveal the reason why.

Like a bolt of lightning, a portion of scripture catapulted out of the night:

…I will very gladly spend and be spent for you…
2 Corinthians 12:15

Spellbound, I listened as God asked me, "If you take all the value out of a dollar bill, what is it worth?"

"Nothing." I said it would only be a useless piece of paper.

"So it is," God replied, "if I take all the sickness, suffering, trials and pain from the life of a child of God." They have nothing to offer, nothing to spend." He spoke again, "Your mother spent it all."

124

When I awoke, I raced to find the words. To spend meant to incur cost. To be spent meant to be totally without resources. The missionaries had bankrupted themselves and their family for the love of their God and the souls of men. When I write these words, you can never imagine the depths of what it means to have your family completely bankrupted. I am not talking about money, but I am talking about the bankrupting of the very *being* of people.

Go and See What They Have Bought With the Price of their Lives

The fog was beginning to lift and the curtain moved back farther this year as God spoke to several people to send me back to the Philippines for the Asian Conference. It had been thirty-eight long

years since I last inhaled that familiar smell through my nostrils and into my lungs and once again saw the sights of what was once my home. I began to see how the seeds that were sown had grown, and the harvest was heavy in the fields. Thank God for all the other missionaries who had come and faithfully labored to continue the work God had started.

While there, we had a one-night crusade and helped pray 682 through to the Holy Ghost. Another night, I was within twenty-five feet of a woman who was healed of a tumor that was supposed to take her life within two months. Another lady who came had no feeling in her legs and arms and was instantly healed and received the Holy Ghost. I saw boys who had been my playmates and had developed into fine men of God, ministers, and presbyters. I talked with elderly men who my dad had baptized. I stood and preached in the very places that my father had preached the great gospel of Jesus Christ.

While there, I traveled into the tombs and found people living there, under the bridges, in cardboard shacks, and along railroad tracks

with only a few inches between their shack and death as railroad cars routinely rolled down the rails.

The Asian Conference was a pre-ministerial training crusade for the pastors and workers. This was the first *Because of the Times Conference* for Asia. The raging fires of revival are burning brightly in the Philippines. China is just a pace away. Yes, I was privileged to be part of this Philippine Dream Team that year, but in reality, **I have been on the Philippine Dream team since I was nine years old in God's eyes.**

Who Believes in You

Take a moment and see if you can name to yourself someone who believes in you. One person who comes to my mind quickly is a mother. A real mother believes in her child. If you went to a mother with a bad report about her child, that mother would have a hard time not defending her child. No! Not my Johnny! And if it was proven that her child did do some terrible deed, the real mother would love her child anyway.

I have a friend who cuts my hair who is probably the best barber in America. He has a naturally up-beat personality which was greatly enhanced when he received the Holy Ghost. One day I went to get a haircut, and the first thing he said to me was, "Thank God for a one-night stand!" This kind of shocked me knowing that he was referring to the time when two people get together who are not married to each other. Of course, he got my attention with that opening line. He went on to say, I know that my mother did not do right, but if it had not been for that encounter, I would not be here, and I would not have the Holy Ghost. The backstory is that my friend was adopted, and his birth mother told his adoptive parents who passed the story down to him that he was the product of a one-night stand. She could have aborted him, but instead she looked for someone to adopt him, so he lived.

In days gone by, the church would shun a young lady if she became pregnant out of wedlock. The child has not done anything to deserve the church's rejection. What the child needs is someone to believe in them. They need someone to come alongside and help them out of the negative environment into which they were born. Having worked in a home for abandoned and neglected children for over a decade and helping in the start-up of an adoption agency, I feel that I know something about the importance for a child of having someone believe in them.

Two are better than one; because they have a good reward for their labour.
For if they fall, the one will lift up his fellow: but woe to him that is alone
when he falleth; for he hath not another to help him up.
Ecclesiastes 4:9-10

Everyone needs someone to believe in them. If no one believes in
me how can I believe in myself? As a spiritual and emotional
caregiver, you certainly have the answer for that. God believes in
you.

There are many reasons why people do not have the strength to
believe in themselves. In one of my corporate chaplain sites, we had
a chicken hatchery. How cute they were with their little beaks and
yellow down. After they were hatched, when the day crew arrived
and started the conveyer belt, the little chicks would be dumped
onto it. As they tumbled and rolled attempting to upright
themselves, they went past a lady who separated them into
different containers to be shipped to the farm where they would
grow for about ninety days before ultimately arriving in their
packages and displayed on your market shelf. What caught my
heart, and the reason why I am including this story, is that this lady
also looked for the unwanted chicks. If one had a deformity or
possibly even a limp, it was whisked off to the "to-be-destroyed
heap." Perhaps the chick had landed wrong when sent down the
chute and hurt its leg. It might have been okay in a few days, but
the lady only had a split second to decide, so off it went to the heap.

God is not a separator who chooses only the perfect. He is a
defender of the fatherless and widow. He is the provider to the poor
and needy. Society will always have the poor, the disadvantaged,
the stepped-on, the abused, injured, and neglected, and those who
seemingly can't get ahead no matter how hard they try.

One phrase I use more than any other when I pray for people,
especially those who are in the hospital is, "God, this is one of your
children lying here …," and always, I feel a sudden relaxing of their
spirit, even when I am praying for a stranger who is of a different
ethnic, cultural, or religious background than myself. Usually I am

holding their hand, and it starts out somewhat ridged, but when I pray those words in their hearing, their hand relaxes, and tears often begin to flow. What did I just do? I was talking to God and said to God, "Here is someone who is important to You; they have worth; they are valuable." In other words, "God, here is someone You believe in, and they need You."

When you no longer believe you are worth anything, and you stop believing in yourself, suicide is a real monster that comes to lurk in the shadows of the mind.

This year, there has already been 895,665 suicides worldwide, and it is only October as I am writing this chapter. Of these, there are twenty-two suicides a day committed by those who are U.S. veterans. It is the tenth leading cause of death in the United States, but more alarming than that, it is the second leading cause of death for those who are ages fifteen to thirty-four. Suicide is at its highest rate since the end of World War II. These statistics are all over the internet. People need the harvesters.

The Painter of Dark Hues

When you minister to humanity with their vast array of issues and problems for very long, you will see the work of the "Dark Painter." How hideous it is as he casts his long shadows over the lives of despondent people and their loved ones. People somehow become convinced when he is telling them that suicide is the right thing to do, or that there is no other way than that direction to which the painted sign points, so they venture onto the shadowy downward path. I am not a psychiatrist nor do I intend to engage in that role, but I am an emotional and spiritual caregiver. I have lived long enough to behold many pictures rendered from the brush of the Dark Painter. As a chaplain, you too will come face to face with suicide and will need some things settled in your heart and mind before you can help others.

I know of an elderly pastor who committed suicide. I do not know all the shades and hues of his life, but I do know some. One of the darker colors was brushed onto the canvas when his wife died not too long previously to his decision. I had ministered at his church a few months before he took his own life. Loneliness is a dark hue, especially in later years. It seems enhanced when a spouse has died. Sickness can add to this as well as some medications. During this time there was a couple in his congregation who began to undermine him and stir up trouble. I had known them from other places where they had also made trouble, and it seemed to be a pattern in their lives. During this time the pastor came to the painted sign and took the self-destructive route as the sign directed, taking his own life with a gun.

Now the question will be asked, "Was he lost?" How can you answer that? As a chaplain or a minister, you will be asked that question, and you will need to be prepared to walk through that minefield. Most of the time it will be someone hurting, looking for hope. Occasionally it will be someone that wants to condemn or justify their own theology.

How do you answer? I do not believe it is a chaplain's job to place a person in heaven or hell. Still, you can give them a directional answer, an answer that neither takes away their hope nor interjects false hope or condemnation. An elder minister I knew put it this way, and I believe it is one of the very best ways to answer this kind of a question; when asked if someone made it to heaven or was lost, he would say, "Why are you asking me to do what God told me not to do? God told us not to judge anything before that day as He will bring all the hidden things to light." Then you can add, "We know that our God is a just and fair God. He will do what is right. Let's leave that in the hands of God." You see, I was not there and do not know what affects the medicine might have had on that pastor. God only knows and He is not telling. I will add that placing someone in hell serves no purpose except to hurt the person who is grieving. It also changes nothing since once they have crossed the line into eternity, there is no changing anything.

Why do people take their own lives? There are so many reasons that I am sure the most highly educated person in this field doesn't know all the reasons. It is safe to say though that there are some basic reasons: loneliness, hopelessness, depression, pride, sickness, mental illness, losing the will to live, and religion, only to name a few.

I bought a book while doing some of my research. I thought it would be about ministering to people on a crisis line who were thinking about suicide. Instead, I received one of the most disgusting books I have ever read and will not name it for this reason. It was so horrible that I only read the first chapter. It was indeed about a crisis hot line for suicide but there was this one volunteer who would not try to dissuade you from killing yourself, but unhesitatingly encouraged it. She would arrange for the caller to meet someone else in the same condition and mindset, and push the two of them to kill themselves together. I was outraged by this and was astonished that a book company would publish such a thing. I cannot imagine how anyone could think this was an acceptable practice or book topic.

In the news in the last few months was a story about a girl who used text messaging to talk her boyfriend into ending his life. What betrayal as she exercised her evil persuasive powers and influenced him to take his own life. I

> ...used text messaging to talk her boyfriend into taking his own life.

wonder what dark delight she got from that. Thank God they prosecuted her for it.

Eddie (not his real name) was a handsome, tall, well-built young man hooked on crack. I had never heard of him nor knew anyone that knew him, but someone had given him my phone number. Before the days of the cell phone, it was the days of the pager. I established a suicide hotline using the pager, then calling them back by phone. At that time, I had a group of about four men who prayed intently for our city. It was on one of those nights of especially intense prayer that we felt the need to drive through the city and pray over different housing projects and apartments. We prayed over several units until we arrived at one particular apartment building where there was a strong feeling to pray. As I remember it, about 3:30 a.m. my phone rang. It was Eddie from that very building where we had felt so strongly to pray. I can still remember the words he spoke. "Preacher, I am getting ready to kill myself." After quite a bit of convincing him that this would not solve his problems, I did what I do not recommend you to do; I arranged to meet him at the Waffle House. After listening to him and talking for a long time, it seemed that the crisis was over, so we parted, agreeing to pick him up for church.

Eddie started coming to church and going to the altar. I had high hopes for him. I went to his home, wanting to teach the Bible and help establish a better course for his family. It was the wife, however, who did not want a change in their home. I well remember her saying, "I have my own religion." Can I tell you it is not about a person's religion; it is about a relationship with Jesus, and this they desperately needed.

132

I was helping Eddie the best I could for several months until one day someone said to me, "Have you heard about Eddie? His wife stabbed him to death last night." What a sad day. To have helped him out of ending his life, only to have it taken by his wife. I do not know what happened that night, but I do know she took his life and went to prison for it.

Those who are hooked on drugs may be seeking help. There are some drug programs and dry-outs that have their places; in-house treatment programs might be somewhat better, but all have a very low success rate. Total healing from drugs has to address the physical, mental, emotional and spiritual needs of the individual. Personally, I believe the one who can bring all of these together is God. I say this from a position of having been delivered from substance abuse myself nearly forty years ago, never to touch it again.

In his book, *Abundant Living*, E. Stanley Jones, the US ambassador to Japan said, "Being a Presbyterian won't stop you from sinning, but it will sure take the fun out of it." [16]His point was, religion is not enough. It takes more than just taking the fun out of what is destroying your life; it takes a change.

The chaplain has many wonderful experiences, but there are sad and disappointing ones as well. When you care you become vulnerable. Any time you love someone, you make yourself vulnerable. Every time your child has fallen and bloodied a knee, it hurt you too. You take upon yourself the heartaches and burdens of those to whom you minister in the same fashion. Chaplains and ministers have to be careful to protect their own emotions and spirituality while ministering to others, else they will not be able to help anyone.

The brush of depression can paint a whole host of dark hues, including but not limited to despondency, hopelessness, aloneness

---

[16] E. Stanley Jones, *Abundant Living*, (New York, NW, Nashville, TN, Abingdon-Cokesbury Press, 1942) 151

133

and despair. Yet, here is a perplexing paradox. The other day I read about a woman who had escaped from North Korea into China three times only to be caught, sent back, taken to prison and tortured. Finally, she escaped and made it to South Korea and now was testifying before the United Nations. In her testimony, she read a poem she had written while in prison.

"I am scared, is anyone there? I'm here in hell, is anyone there? I scream and yell but no one opens the door. Is anyone there? Please listen to our moans and listen to our pain. Is anyone there? People are dying, my friend is dying. I call out again and again but why don't you answer. Is anyone there?" Written by Ji Hyeon-A, a North Korean defector. [17]Here you have a woman who is desperately trying to live, eating rats and locusts to survive, struggling against great odds that would depress just about anyone, yet in all of her struggles, sufferings, neglect and torture, she is trying to live.

On the other hand, we have the Aokigahara forest in Japan where people go to commit suicide on the average of two a week. What is the difference? Why are people who are not oppressed by their government, are not sent to prison for trying to escape, are not tortured, neglected or deprived, killing themselves and why there? The Painter of Dark Hues has been at his work again.

One theory is that the site was made popular by a novel, *Kurio Jukai,* about two lovers who end up committing suicide in that forest. Another was the book *The*

---

[17] Ben Evansky, Fox News. North Korean Defector, Ji Hyeon-A, describes forced abortion, said bodies fed to dogs in prison. Published December 11, 2017

Complete Manual to Suicide by Wataru Tsurumi in which he says that Aokigahara forest is "the perfect place to die and end all pain."

Japan has a unique culture that exerts immense pressure on its people to perform and excel above and beyond other nations. It is their philosophy that to fail is a shame, a shame on your family, yourself, and even your community and country.

In an article in the New York Times, Feb 22, 2018, Jonathan Kaiman tells of a set of cliffs about two hundred miles from Tokyo where people go to commit suicide by jumping eighty feet into the sea. He tells of a retired policeman who daily tries to find and stop people from killing themselves. One young lady he found told him that she had not done her homework and was embarrassed. Instead of going to school that day, she had ridden the bus and then the train two hundred miles intending to kill herself on these cliffs. This policeman talked her out of killing herself that day and called her parents, asking them, "What is more important, her school or her life?" How sad that he had to even ask that question.

Being bullied is a great tragedy. It hits hardest on the young who cannot yet bear up under the blows of their peers. A simple message of, "You are important; you are someone special, you are loved," could help stop many suicides. But the bullies say, "You are not worth anything; you are ugly; no one wants to be with you; no one likes you." I am thinking of a young girl who threw herself off of an overpass onto moving cars because she believed she wasn't worth anything.

Pride can lead to suicide. When the stock market fell in 1929, some wealthy people jumped out of high-rise buildings at the thought of losing everything

> Religious suicides are…among the strongest forces for ending one's life.

Religious suicides are some of the most wasteful and ignorant of all suicides. Religious suicides are also one of the most deceitful and among the strongest forces for ending one's life. James Town and the Rev. Jim Jones stand out where misled brainwashed people all died together, fathers, mothers and children. Some may have been forced, but almost all died willfully.

Heaven's Gate cult is another example where educated people were convinced that they were destined to die and meet an extraterrestrial spacecraft following the comet Hale-Bopp. Thirty-nine died together.

Suicide bombers are captivated by the dark hues painted onto a religious canvas, dark hues that promise an afterlife of wondrous reward for those who give the ultimate sacrifice to save their people from the suffering injustices perpetrated by outsiders. Since this philosophy is taught beginning with children, it is nearly impossible to reverse their thinking, if you would even have access to them, however, you might be called to minister to victims of such tragedies as what occurred at the World Trade Center on September 11, 2001.

Many times chaplains are called to help the survivors. Their questions are sincere and full of pain. Especially in cases of suicide, they ask, "Is it our fault? What did we do wrong? If only I had…" The ministry of presence is very important in times like this. Just being there and letting the victims talk is a great comfort to them. Don't get caught up in trying to answer all the questions. They are often not looking for you to answer anyway. Mostly they are merely trying to sort through it in their mind. Regret and self-blame are a trap for them. Grieving is right, but self-blame is dangerous. In most cases I have no problem assuring the grieving left behind that it was not their fault. It may be someone's fault, say in the case of bullying, but not the grieving loved ones. I might say something like, "Perhaps they had gotten to the point where they were not thinking straight enough to imagine how much this was going to hurt you. But, I am sure they would not want you to think that it was your fault." The person who commits suicide makes that decision themselves in most cases.

One of the things to watch for is copy-cat suicide. I was dealing with a man whose wife's mother went into her barn, strung up some plastic so as not to make a big mess, and killed herself with a shotgun. The man's wife had become very depressed. As his chaplain, I had offered to help, but he thought her church was helping her. This continued for several months until she progressed to the place that she would not even get out of bed or leave the house. These were signs that she needed greater professional assistance which I don't believe she received. In the end she committed suicide as her mother had also done. The chaplain must be aware of the signs that a person needs greater professional help and do a follow-up to make sure the person receives the help that they need.

Then there is the unexplained and unexpected suicide. Not too long ago I was asked to help a couple who lost their son as a result of suicide. There were no signs of anything being wrong. There was no known strain in his relationship with his parents, siblings or co-workers. There were no recent relationship break-ups and the young man was just getting ready to launch into a new exciting job. This was a God-fearing, church-involved, loving family, this son included. Suddenly, without warning, their son was gone. This left the family with so many unanswered questions. What did we do wrong? Why did he not come talk with us? Why did this happen? Mostly, I just let them talk, only asking a few questions to clarify my own understanding of the events. Sometimes all you can do is just be there and listen to their sorrows.

This chapter was not meant to be an in-depth training on how to help suicidal people, for there are many great places to obtain training which would be necessary if you feel a calling into that ministry. Perhaps you might consider joining a suicide crisis line or even start one. Chaplain training is a lifelong pursuit in which you need special training to prepare you to meet the needs of others.

Give instruction to a wise man, and he will be yet wiser:
teach a just man, and he will increase in learning.
Proverbs 9:9

What I Believe

When ministering to people, a chaplain must minister in Christian love to all people regardless of faith. A sincere respect for others and their faith or lack thereof is a must. They must faithfully attend to people who have no faith in God at all, haters of God, the agnostics, un-believers, and Christians. Yet in all that you do to look after the spiritual and emotional needs of others as a caregiver, you cannot let go of your own belief in God, His teachings, or your own testimony. Offering others what you have in God is the only *real* hope you have to offer the broken of this world. You are neither a psychologist nor a psychiatrist, so your ministry is not to analyze people. As a caregiver, you offer emotional support for what they are going through, and you give them spiritual support, showing them they can turn to God any time.

To that end I take this space to explain what I hold to be true. I believe that Jesus was the Son of God, yet He was much more than just the Son. The Son-ship of Jesus was His fleshly body, but what was on the inside was God Almighty. This is borne out of **Isaiah 9:6** as well as **John 1:1-14** and many other places in the Bible. Because God is a Spirit and has not a body, the only physical representation we will see sitting on the throne in Heaven will be the glorified body of our Lord Jesus Christ who is the express image of God. (**Hebrews,** the first chapter).

Believing is the first step of salvation but not the only step. **John 1:12** says that in *receiving him* we are given the right to *become the sons of God*. I know that there is a need for people to repent so that their sins can be forgiven, yet it is in the waters of baptism that the sins are washed away. This is the act that Paul says is the circumcision of the heart *made without hands,* **Colossians 2:8-12**, the body of sin, the old nature, being cut off as we are buried in baptism and resurrected by faith.

The promise of the Father, which is the Holy Ghost, is for everyone as prophesied in **Joel 2** and is what happened in **Acts 2**. It is a baptism of the power from on high, commonly called the baptism of the Holy Ghost. This gives us power to become witnesses for Him.

The Word of God tells us that God is no respecter of persons, so He will give you the Holy Ghost if you will obey Him. I believe He still heals today, miracles are still performed by Him, and all things are possible to those who believe.

...with God all things are possible
Matthew 19:26

I believe that He will return, and if I am alive, I will go to meet Him in the air, and if I should be dead, He will raise me up to life again.

A Challenge to You

As we are nearing the end of our time together, I want to thank you for reading what I have written. But it needs to be more than just a book you have read. I want to challenge you to reach out and take hold of the dark cover that hides the reefs in the shadowy waters of your life's sea. Rip off that cover and look into the sea again and face the unpleasant things that hide below the surface. The disappointments, hurts, unjust treatment, and wrongs done to you are living in the rocky reef. Face it all. Be prepared for an emotional time, but it will be worth it as it will free you. Be desperately honest with yourself. Hear your own story; no, not the one you tell others but the real story. Cry if you must, and pray, but don't let the creatures go back to hide in the darkness.

Sometimes, you may have to take your past hurtful memories in small segments like a friend of mine did. It took him several years to come to grips with the realization that not only had his father abused him, but his mother had also. His mind seemed to block many things from his memory and would only allow more details to surface as he could handle it.

Most people who care deeply enough to help others have themselves been deeply hurt. Dr. Joyce Langdorf Heatherley, in her book, *Irregular People*,[18] tells the story of her irregular person, and only when she faced the hurt in her life was she able to get free from its prison. I recommend Joyce's book.

This is entirely Biblical.

> *And ye shall know the truth,*
> *and the truth shall make you free.*
> **John 8:32**

Once you face your own uncomfortable memories, then you are better able to help someone else.

---

[18] Joyce Landorf Heatherley, *Irregular People*, (Georgetown, TX, Balcony Publishing, Inc., 1988)

In conclusion, if you have a need in your life, emotionally or spiritually, and would like someone to talk with you about it, you can use the contact information below, and I will arrange for someone to listen. If you would like someone to pray for you, please contact us; someone does care. Especially contact us if you feel you are at the end of your rope and are thinking about giving up.

If you would like more information about chaplain training and endorsement, you can contact me using the contact information below.

Web Site: www.ocachaplains.com

Email: William@plisolutions.com

About the Author

William Dillon started chaplain work over 40 years ago in a Union Gospel Mission, eventually progressing from member to president. While president a battered women's program was started and that was just the beginning. Currently, he is the director of the Occupational Chaplains Association which has trained and endorsed hundreds of chaplains.

On his quest for skills to help others, he has served as Christian Prisoner Fellowship (CPF) state and regional director, been a police chaplain having completed law enforcement chaplain training, served seven years as corporate chaplain, and numerous years a hospital chaplain. He has also been a Justice Court chaplain, and worked in drug rehabilitation programs and federal halfway houses. Additionally, he is a Drug and Alcohol Instructor and an Anger Management Instructor.

Chaplain Dillon completed the first unit of Clinical Pastoral Education and has pastored churches in Washington state and Arkansas, and assisted in other churches when not pastoring his own. He would say, with the help of God he advanced. Now he would like to share stories and some of what he has learned to help give you tools for your ministry.

He currently makes Tupelo, Mississippi his home.

Shouldest not thou also have had compassion on thy fellowservant, even as I had pity on thee?
Matthew 18:33